Women
in Medical Education

Women in Medical Education

An Anthology of Experience

EDITED BY

Delese Wear

State University of New York Press

Published by
State University of New York Press, Albany

© 1996 State University of New York

Printed in the United States of America

"The Feminization of Medicine," from *Baby Doctor* by Perri Klass. Copyright © 1992 by Perri Klass. Reprinted by permission of Random House, Inc.
"Feminist Criticism in Literature and Medicine," by Delese Wear. Copyright © 1994 by Alpha Omega Alpha Honor Medical Society. Reprinted by permission from *The Pharos*, Volume 57, Number 4.

For information, address State University of New York Press, State University Plaza, Albany, N.Y., 12246

Production by Diane Ganeles
Marketing by Dana Yanulavich

Library of Congress Cataloging-in-Publication Data

Women in medical education : an anthology of experience / Delese Wear, editor.
    p.   cm.
  Includes bibliographical references and index.
  ISBN 0-7914-3087-1 (cloth : alk. paper). – ISBN 0-7914-3088-X (pbk. : alk. paper)
    1. Women in medicine. 2. Medical teaching personnel. I. Wear, Delese.
  R692W.656 1996
  610.82–dc20   95-49902
                                                                    CIP

10 9 8 7 6 5 4 3 2 1

Contents

III. Personal and Professional Identities

Foreword

❑

Frances K. Conley

This anthology of experience provides a historical reference point at a pivotal time for medicine in the United States. The stated goal of the enterprise was daunting enough—explore medicine, humanities, and feminism and bring them together as an amalgamated whole between the cover of a single book. That the task remains unfinished has more to do with history, than in minimizing the contributions of the varied writers—indeed, their thoughts, shared stories, and emotionality are compelling, convincing, and ring with the necessity to forge ahead, to wherever that may lead. The common concern, articulated by all, is that a culture shift must occur, a rigid structure become moldable or broken, or abolished. However, lessons from the history of modern medicine do not indicate the correct choice as to how, and by whom, the structure will be altered. After all, hierarchical structure is a fact of human life, politically, economically, and psychologically. Hierarchy has served medicine well; its patriarchy is caring, if not compassionate, technically proficient, if not emotionally involved. So we are left with the written uncertainties of these pioneers; their doubts, anxieties, their victimization by a system they think they understand only too well but which has yet to live up to its promises to them. The human spirit absorbs absolute oppression, but revolts over unmet expectations, and this collection of writings represents a tentative revolution.

To date, the medical world has successfully avoided any but the most superficial of scrutiny by both groups—humanists and feminists. Both are foreign and feared, but for different reasons. Feminism because it is thought of primarily in terms of women, and as women gain in numbers, if not stature, within medicine, where are the men, and who will think of (and for) them? Humanism because the discipline deliberately asks the unanswerable, forces physicians to think about that which is uncomfortable, because, increasingly, unlike their traditional medical education, there is no "right" answer. The humanists make sport of the rigid "science" in medicine, the bulwark of the profession, the mystical knowledge base that undergirds a practitioner's right to declare, "Father knows best, little girl, what you need and is right for you." The imprecision of such scrutiny, along with the double dose of effect, has no place in the medical structure, where "the doctor" in male guise, has ruled for centuries, secure in power and control. Not so strange, then, these questions and criticisms may well be discarded, minimized, placated, ignored. The institution under siege, after all, protects "life," not some business endeavor or legal nicety.

As readers we are treated to a treatise of struggle, stories of an uneasy "fit" in a world that still doesn't really want them, stories of marked uncertainty of how, or even whether, to proceed, what is the next step. How can the message be crafted so as to reach every physician—male, female, minority—with the same impact and expectation of similarity in response? The medical world will deny their right to exist as humanists and/or women, but grudgingly will consider assimilation of both if there is agreement to adhere to rigid rules patterned by the patriarchy. And perhaps that is the most important message of these writers, themselves full of uneasiness, anxiety and even apology, the message that the largest fear is assimilation, and with assimilation death of the right, or need to question a revered structure, a grateful slide into the morass of complacency, a willingness to accept, yet again, "business as usual."

At no time in the history of modern medicine have so many been there eroding the absolute authority of the male physician—economists, politicians, insurance companies, nurses, patients, humanists, and women. He is losing control of his once sacrosanct world where he, and only he, dictated its modus operandi. By itself, medicine cannot reform a world where everywhere women work harder to earn less, accept responsibility for family at the price of oppression, where female life is not valued as highly as male life. The United States will train many women doctors, good, compassionate doctors, and medical education will include the female species. I have no doubt about all of this. However, inequities will persist, and the need for feminists (defined in the broadest of terms) and humanists to question continues. Our women medics will fill a crying need for primary care physicians in health maintenance organizations—at low prestige and low pay. Just as "nurse" today is "woman," so will "primary care doctor" tomorrow be "woman." These professional women won't worry about the fit of their suit; a dress with ruffles will be just fine. Hierarchical control will persist, not in excluding women from medicine in the time-honored tradition, but in determining their type of practice. The male doctor will rule by control of the highly paid, prestigious specialty practices, which again, will exclude those deemed incompatible (read different). The struggle, disguised, is still there, but it will be different, thus the historical value of this collection of essays at this point in time. We can only hope that question, inquiry, and recording into and about the saga continue.

Introduction

I have often thought that medical education and feminism seem incompatible: a woman cannot be affiliated or identify with both. But if she manages to do so, she might find it difficult to enact them simultaneously. And because one is a job description with rules, norms, and boundaries for acceptable beliefs and behaviors, and the other a political project often working at oppositional angles to those very practices, she may be inclined to regulate her feminism—or have it regulated for her.

I have been in medical education for over a decade and have been thinking and writing about women in medicine for many of those years. I am a student of my women students as I watch them with deep respect and sometimes puzzlement. I respect their intelligence and skills; their willingness to (nearly) martyr themselves to care for others in one of the most dramatic, time-intensive of all professions; their attempts to meld this consuming work with lives outside medicine; and their efforts to do so in settings that are implicitly and explicitly coded by gender, race, social class, and ethnic identity. Yet I am puzzled by many of these same women as students and later as faculty colleagues who manage to work (and yes, even thrive) in settings where middle- and upper-class, well-educated and paid, usually white men are the policy-makers, procedure-doers, and attention-getters; where working-class, frequently poorly educated and paid, often women of color clean the medical schools, hospital rooms, and patients themselves. I am perplexed because I see them engaged in very little sustained critique of this overtly patriarchic foundation of academic medicine that sorts many of them and other women out of career choices and rewards, and prevents many of them from a meaningful integration of their professional and personal selves. Spending one's work life in such an environment has resulted in many women in medicine living with a fair amount of frustration and yes, anger.

Of course there are moments of critique. Thanks to women like Stanford neurosurgeon Frances Conley who publicly confronted the insidious and too often unchallenged sexism in her own context; or Janet Bickel of the Association of American Medical Colleges who has spent years tracking women physicians'/scientists' career patterns in medical education, there are some institutional gestures toward confronting these immense inequities and injustices.

Likewise, because of the growing number of women in medicine, residency programs are beginning to think about and even implement maternity/parental leave policies; women are finding themselves in medical specialties hugely underrepresented by women; and women are finding more and more of those whom Leah Dickstein calls "men of good conscience" who call themselves feminist, who are willing to confront violations that others claim "will just take time" to erase.

This book is an openly ideological, partial, and unfinished project of women coming together to tell stories—their own—and to theorize variously about women, doctoring, medicine, knowledge, power, families, the academy, patriarchy. As editor, I asked each contributor to write a personal narrative about her feminism—its forms, promises, and problems; and to describe how she enacts her feminism in medical school or university settings and in her life outside medicine.

The essays that followed this request were as diverse as the women who wrote them. Narratives emerged from basic science and clinical settings; at undergraduate and graduate levels across disciplines; in the medical academy and in hospital settings; in their daily, formal and informal encounters with students, peers, administrators, and patients; at home with families. These contributors frequently critiqued the encompassing, deeply embedded, and often unexamined hierarchical foundation of medical education that pervades its structure and intellectual practices.

This is charting new ground. While it is true that feminist philosophers of science have been engaged in a vigorous debate surrounding the implicit ideological basis of western, Enlightenment-based scientific thought for many years (Harding 1986; Haraway 1988; Lather 1991), we find no corresponding radical critique of the *foundational* underpinnings of the medical academy. Indeed, up to this point most feminist debate in academic medicine has been framed to keep women on the defensive, working *within* the existing institutional framework by "offering hope for improvement—but only if they did not rock the patriarchal boat too vigorously" (Warren 1992, 34). Working within a prescribed arena keeps debate surrounding gender (or race, or national origins) away from the larger foundational critique of an institution—here, the medical academy—that continues to operate on unequal power relationships. Susan Sherwin points out that the silence has been deafening on the patriarchal practice of medicine, that "the deep questions about the structure of medical practice and its role in a patriarchal society are largely inaccessible within the [existing] framework" (1992, 23).

No such fainthearted critique here. Indeed, these authors' refusal to remain silent, the values and practices they question, and their ability to use language other than the "arcane, technically precise, esoteric language of the intellectual elite" (Yeatman 1994, 195), make them subaltern intellectuals in the medical academy. That is, they are positioned across audiences: the people they write for are not just those who have the power to determine and advance their academic careers, but include those who want to talk feminism or other forms of activism in order to become the kinds of service-delivery practitioners they want to be, as well as activists within the community outside the academy (Yeatman, 195).

An explication of terms and methods is in order. First, the use of "feminism" or "feminist." I had no desire to search for an unproblematic, universal definition of the term. The authors found here differ widely in their insider/outsider status in academic hierarchies, their beliefs about the nature of social change, and the character of their activism. I do, however, share Susan Sherwin's belief that there are some core views that transcend the divergencies that separate feminists in their internal debates, views the contributors found here share. These common themes include a "recognition that women are in a subordinate position in society, that oppression is a form of injustice and hence is intolerable, that there are further forms of oppression in addition to gender oppression (and that there are women victimized by each of these forms of oppression), that it is possible to change society in ways that could eliminate oppression, and that it is a goal of feminism to pursue the changes necessary to accomplish this" (1992, 29).

Second, method. This book rests on the authority of experience, a current in feminist theorizing that dismantles the public-private dichotomy and refuses the theoretical evacuation of the writer. With the exception of the first three writers who provide overviews of the presence, status, and some major concerns of women in medicine, the contributors to this volume recognize that personal and political disengagement and value-neutrality is neither possible nor desirable in this undertaking. Their writing is personal criticism, an "explicitly autobiographical performance . . . [a] self-narrative woven into critical argument" (Miller 1991, 1-2). They write not as self-indulgent confessionals to evoke sympathy or outrage, but to illuminate our collective yet localized struggles, and to work collectively and collaboratively to end ways of knowing, structures of power, medical role-playing, and distribution of resources that oppress and exploit women and others.

Here is the task: how to begin, how to order the theme(s) of feminism in medical education, written by women across disciplines, locations, social arrangements, life histories. The first division is apparent. Three essays by Leah Dickstein, Janet Bickel, and Delese Wear provide readers with historical and theoretical perspectives of women in medicine. Dickstein, whose leadership and mentorship have been invaluable to a whole generation of women physicians, provides an overview of women in medicine in the United States. Bickel, who has from her vantage point at the Association of American Medical Colleges perhaps the most comprehensive view of women's career patterns in medicine and medical education in North America, has written a national perspective on sexism and professional development in medicine. Finally, Wear and Bickel ground their chapter in the results of a survey of women faculty appointed as liaison officers to the Association of American Medical Schools, discussing this groups' perceptions of feminism and the climate in which they work.

A second group of essays focuses on training and workplace issues outside family and parenting concerns. I make this distinction with hesitation, not wishing to imply a tidy division between our lives at work and our lives as members of families and communities. Still, five essays focus more directly on environmental issues rather than the pressures of these other commitments. Jacalyn Duffin traces her professional development as a physician *and* a historian, describing what that has meant to her medical career, how it has influenced her teaching, and how it has helped her to realize that our "failure to contemplate . . . what it has meant to be a 'doctor' [is] a product of centuries of male definition." Mary Mahowald writes on how idealist pragmatism informs her work, and provides examples of how she survives and even sometimes prospers in a medical academy. "Father Knows Best . . ." is the wry title of Deborah Jones's essay that traces the development of her feminist consciousness, a consciousness that helped her to focus a critique of sexist structures in the medical academy, including exclusionary/segregationary networking, language patterns, environmental arrangements, and other differential treatment of women. Dale Blackstock adds the story of her journey from the inner city to Harvard Medical School, drawing strength along the way from her family and mentors and looking now to her mother and other African American women who have "achieved the unachievable." Perri Klass draws on her own experience along with other well-known women physicians to address the question, "Do Women Make Better Doctors?" Next, Kate Brown describes what her feminist commitments mean to teaching ethics and health policy: "something forged from the dynamic swirl of political and economic influences which need to be appreciated and weighed in light of one's moral and medical judgments, upbringing, personal commitments, and emotional state." Pamela Charney describes her innovative efforts to develop a combined residency program in general internal medicine and women's health. "Life as a Sheep in the Cow's Pasture" is how Marian Gray Secundy describes her life as an African-American feminist in the predominantly black environment of Howard University. And finally, I have written an essay that proposes how feminist criticism might become a framework for teaching literature in medical settings, whereby issues illuminated by literature take readers deeper into the personal and political domains, where teachers and students together can engage in heretical questioning of patriarchal practices in both the culture at large and in the medical culture reflecting and reinforcing those practices.

A third section, "Personal and Professional Identities," includes essays in which writers bring to the foreground more of their lives outside medicine to examine the importance and uneraseable presence of those lives in the dailiness of their work as doctors, researchers, teachers. Rebekah Wang-Cheng weaves stories of her mother—a woman born in China in 1912 and "a feminist who probably doesn't even know the meaning of the word"—throughout her essay as a reminder to feminists in medical education to lead the way in demonstrating respect for others as well as for ourselves. Like Wang-Cheng, both Lucy Candib and Beth Alexander include parenting issues in their personal narratives as physicians. Alexander's essay, written as diary entries beginning with her application to medical school when she was already a mother and a counselor, weaves incidents and observations about patients, doctors, gender, and power, often returning to the seeming impasse of finding herself torn between her own needs, the expectations of her job, the needs of her patients, and the needs of her children. Candib's essay contains a running dialogue/interrogation between the formal content of her written text and her thoughts about the process, braiding stories of her doctoring in a neighborhood health center, teaching residents, laboring through childcare issues with residents and colleagues, and still, twenty years after she started to practice, working against medicine "trying to make a man" out of her. And last, Marjorie Sirridge writes of her long journey through medicine, working through a training system never intended for women with children, and discovering several men of good conscience along the way who helped her acquire the credentials that marked the beginning of a extraordinary fifty-year career in medicine and medical education.

I believe the theoretical/political, methodological, and practical issues surrounding gender are complex, historically situated, and tangled in the influence of a language we only partially understand. Like bell hooks (1992), I think the kind of theorizing found here

> invites readers to engage in critical reflection and in the practice of feminism. To me, this theory emerges from [our] efforts to make sense of everyday life experiences . . . Our search leads us back to where it all began, to that moment when a woman or child, who may have thought she was all alone, began feminist uprising, began to name her practice, began to formulate theory from experience. (82)

The styles, stories, and situations of the writers found here reflect these complexities; their context-bound subjectivities will quickly become apparent to readers. Moreover, their differences even in the face of their common commitments are illustrative of feminism itself, and, I hope, part of the multilayered feminist consciousness found and evolving in the medical academy.

PART I

Historical and Theoretical Perspectives

CHAPTER 1

Overview of Women Physicians
in the United States

❑

Leah J. Dickstein

Their History

The March 1995 issue of *The New Physician* published by the American Medical Student Association (AMSA) was a special issue entitled, "Women Add a New Dimension to Medicine." Topics included: the number of women medical students, sexual harassment, pregnancy and parenting from the medical student through resident and faculty perspective, the dearth of senior women physicians in leadership roles (the "Lexan Ceiling"), mentoring, the history of women physicians, the current situation of women physicians worldwide, and the current and emerging knowledge and lack of sufficient research concerning women's health. Several articles were authored by men, including one by AMSA's president, Terrence Steyer, M.D., 1994. The latter was most appropriately sensitive to the issues already listed.

In January 1995, a final draft was approved of the *Fifth Report: Women and Medicine* for the Council on Graduate Medical Education (COGME). This landmark report, published by the Department of Health and Human Services for Congress, will be available for public access. The report included a chapter I wrote, "Status of Women Physicians in the Workforce," with data compiled by a Brown University medical student, Daniel P. Dickstein, and initial comments and contributions to the bibliography given by Carol C. Nadelson, professor of psychiatry at Harvard and Tufts University.

The current president of the Association of American Medical Colleges, Jordan Cohen, was appointed in 1994. In March 1995, he sent a memo to the Council of Deans, copying Women Liaison Officers and Minority Affairs Section, requesting nominees for senior positions including names of women and under-represented minorities in academic medicine who could and would want to be promoted to senior leadership roles as department chairs and full deans. He wrote, "I believe the time has come for us to make *explicit* efforts to level the playing field."

Why is this national, highly visible focus on women in medicine occurring now? The answers to this question can best be garnered by looking at where we have been.

Most people interested in the history of women physicians in the United States know about Elizabeth Blackwell, first a schoolteacher in northern Kentucky in order to help her family, and then better known as the first woman physician to graduate from a co-educational medical school—Geneva Medical College in New York State—in 1847. But few know of Mrs. Frances Coomes, Kentucky's first woman physician who, because of religious discrimination, came with her husband William from Maryland and then the Virginias in the 1770s to Fort Harrod, Kentucky. She apprenticed to a male physician to learn medicine. Another student served his apprenticeship at the same time; he was later known as *Dr.* John Hart. Mrs. Coomes, also the first schoolteacher in Kentucky, taught in a one-room log cabin schoolhouse that remains preserved in Fort Harrod's museum; there is no obvious record there of her medical career. There are, however, early written records by John Ouchterlony (1890) of Mrs. Coomes' medical expertise, including reports of her orthopedic surgery prowess in restoring function to her grandson's clubfoot and in treating male patients who sought her professional care from as far away as the Virginias.

Several excellent sources detail the early history of women physicians in the United States: *Sympathy and Science* by Regina Morantz-Sanchez (1985); *Physicians Wanted: No Women Need Apply* by Mary Roth Walsh (1977); and *Hospital With A Heart* by Virginia Drachman (1984). In essence, the "her" story is that women as physicians were not generally truly wanted or accepted; rather, the role of nurse-midwife was their proper place. During the Civil War, Mary Walker, served as a physician disguised as a man. In the later 1800s following Elizabeth Blackwell's accomplishment to achieve mainstream medical education, she, together with her physician sister Emily, opened the New York Infirmary for Women and an adjacent medical school for women.

Many medical colleges, including homeopathic schools, opened for training women because of their continued exclusion from existing schools. The number of women physicians increased until the 1910 Flexner Report for the Carnegie Foundation, which outlined more rigorous expectations and requirements for medical education. Consequently, many schools closed, and the ones that remained did not welcome women students on an equitable basis. In fact, Woman's Medical College of Pennsylvania remained the only all-women medical school in the United States from 1910 until 1970.

At other institutions, women were accepted in very small numbers based upon unspoken quotas. Harvard first accepted women as medical students in 1945 because of the shortage of male students during World War II; their unspoken and unwritten quota remained at a maximum of six percent of each entering class until the mid-1970s. If there were few women medical students (perhaps two or three per class), there were even fewer women physician faculty, especially at senior leadership levels. For those women pioneers who endured less than full status as students in clinical opportunities, obtaining an internship prolonged their struggle with inequality. Most hospitals would not accept women trainees, thus the need for hospitals where women could train and also treat women patients. There were fewer women trained as physicians *after* the Flexner Report, a trend that did not change until the 1970s.

For African-American women professionals, opportunities were even fewer. Sarah Fitzbutler, wife of physician Henry Fitzbutler, helped him open and administer the Louisville National Medical College in 1892. When Henry died, Sarah had already become a physician and ran the school until Flexner Report repercussions caused the school's closing in 1912. Two of their daughters, Mary and Prima, obtained their medical training at Woman's Medical College in Philadelphia.

The American Medical Women's Association (AMWA) was organized in Chicago in 1915 by Bertha VanHoosen, a local gynecologist-surgeon who had first worked in a state psychiatric hospital as a psychiatrist. She was joined with several other women physician colleagues who were determined to form a medical organization when the American Medical Association (AMA), also located in Chicago, persisted in denying them membership.

The Current Situation

As a consequence of the second wave of feminism which began in the mid-1960s, increasing numbers of women began to apply and be accepted into medical schools beginning in the mid-1970s. Their numbers rose quickly from six to eight percent of the class to twenty to thirty percent in the 1980s, and in the mid-1990s at least a dozen schools have enrolled more women than men (Bickel, Galbraith, and Quinnie 1995).

Many of the women students who have gained admittance since the surge in the mid-1970s have not only been academically superior students applying directly from college, but they have included increasing numbers of women who had other jobs and careers, like nurses or teachers, or were full-time homemakers. Many had always aspired to becoming physicians, but felt external and personal barriers were insurmountable. Up until this precipitous rise, a substantial number of women who entered careers as physicians did so with the support of fathers who lacked sons; many of these were their families' oldest or only children.

The syndrome of "substitute son" has all but evaporated in comparison to the numbers of women from all walks of life, from all personal backgrounds and with a variety of college majors who have successfully challenged admission committees with equally admirable academic and extracurricular records. These women medical students, whether in their twenties, thirties or forties, have also challenged themselves to succeed, often and understandably believing and feeling they had to work twice as hard to succeed. They also believed, with good reason, that greater opportunities for the next classes of women depended upon their current group's performances.

Not surprisingly, many of these women consistently ranked at the top and often were first in their graduating classes, also appropriately receiving many of the academic prizes. Many who were both uninformed or uninterested in the problems for women in medicine were surprised at the earned accomplishments of these women; others resented their presence; some felt threatened.

One situation which has always existed for women physicians and persists even today is that women have been overly encouraged and mentored to enter primary care fields where they can enhance patient care by using their more acknowledged skills of better communication with patients. They have clearly and simultaneously been discouraged from applying to train in the more technical and higher remunerative fields of the subspecialties of surgery and medicine. Fortunately, these barriers are beginning to decrease and disappear. In 1994 for the first time ever, more women than men entered training programs in obstetrics and gynecology.

Despite twenty-five years of a substantial increase in the number of women physicians, women are less likely to have achieved parity with their male peers at the same level in salary for the same work, whether in practice or in academia. In academic medicine, they are also less likely to have achieved the same academic rank as their male peers, and they have assumed proportionately fewer leadership roles as full deans and department chairs, division chiefs and hospital administrators in medical schools. If they do achieve the rank of full professor, it takes them on average twenty rather than twelve years to reach that level.

As of 1995, female department chairs in medical schools numbered in single digits in each specialty except pediatrics (11) and family practice (12). Currently there is only one woman chair of internal medicine, the very field that contains the largest number of women physicians. The largest number of women department chairs exists in the newest field of family practice; the next largest is in pediatrics.

Although large numbers of women have always joined psychiatry departments, currently only three chairs are women. There are now three women full deans, though one is stepping down. There have been a few others in the past decade, but only for very short time periods. Although there have been up to several women national presidents of specialty and subspecialty societies and of local medical organizations, the expectation that this will continue has not yet been accepted.

I have described the major barrier in women reaching and assuming senior leadership roles as the effect of the Lexan ceiling. Lexan is a bulletproof plastic which at 1/4 inch is stronger than steel. Thus, women cannot break through the assumed glass ceiling, but instead must collaborate with "men of good conscience," i.e., men with power and understanding that women can and should assume leadership roles. The ceiling must be removed by women and men working together. What must also be recognized is that many women lead differently from the "ladder style" of most men (Dickstein 1991).

Projections for the Future

Common sense, optimism and a belief in gender equity should converge to predict and hope for the continuing increase of women physicians to impact more positively with more opportunities in every area and aspect in medicine.

In 1993 the Congressional Caucus for Women's Issues, a coalition of women members of Congress, included in their report recommendations to recognize and work to eliminate gender bias toward women physicians and their women patients. This was called the Women's Health Equity Act. In 1992 the National Institutes of Health's Office of Research on Women's Health directed by Vivian Pinn, a pathologist and former chair at Howard, and the Society for the Advancement of Women's Health Research held a number of forums nationwide to develop plans to increase the role of women scientists in medical research. This latter factor had many facets because more research must be conducted on women and more women should be doing this research.

Furthermore, more primary care physicians are projected to be needed in the next few years and into the twenty-first century. Women physicians' personal lives are not becoming easier to direct and implement, and issues of sexual harassment and gender bias remain potent negative forces for too many women.

Problems Encountered by Women Physicians Which Must Be Addressed for Prevention, Elimination and Remediation

This final section will focus on each of the major problems women continue to face as they pursue their careers in medicine. Elimination of these problems must be understood to be the responsibility of women and men based on attitudes and values reflected in society, respect for differences and consideration of factors at first glance not necessarily directly connected to medicine.

Gender bias in medicine, or the attitude, value and belief reflected in behavior toward and about women by men and women is that they are less worthy than men to pursue a medical career and to have equal opportunities in every medical area of education, training, research and practice. Gender bias must be recognized and eliminated by constant oversight by the most powerful in medicine because despite its being against the law, it still exists in blatant and subtle ways and impedes women's achievements and all their activities.

Sharon Lenhart, a physician who is Vice President for Career Development of the American Medical Women's Association, has written that gender bias "constitutes gender discrimination when behaviors, actions, policies, procedures or interactions adversely affect a woman's work due to disparate treatment, disparate impact or the creation of a hostile or intimidating work environment (Lenhart 1993). Gender bias can include unfair, outmoded expectations and assumptions about women which are used as the basis for decision-making regarding the women without discussing the issues with them directly.

The opposite of gender bias, i.e., gender equity, is the type of attitude and behavior toward women which must take its rightful place in all aspects of attitudes, judgments and behaviors toward women. One effort to bring gender equity into the mainstream of medicine (particularly for women) was the creation in 1993 of the American Medical Women's Association Faculty Gender Equity Awards supported by the Upjohn Company. This annual award is available at every medical school to be given to a preclinical and clinical faculty member selected by the women and men medical students for their gender equity toward women and men students. Recognizing appropriate behavior is clearly one way to reinforce positive efforts and change; and with appropriate publicity, the message can be sent to all colleagues that changing behavior can be rewarding.

Other issues, such as provision of time and opportunity to bear and raise children as a part of a normal life for women and men, must be recognized and not punished. Available, high quality child care in proximity to training and practice sites can be invaluable to those in need. Allowing appropriate time to care for children and other significant dependents must be seen as natural and humane and not professionally detrimental over an entire career.

Mentoring by senior men who continue to outnumber senior women must be seen as vital to junior women students, residents, faculty and those who have recently entered practice. True mentoring does not consist of over-control or of decisions made by the mentor for and about the mentee without discussion and listening. Opportunities in research, training and clinical practice must be offered to women on an equal basis with men without destructive assumptions and gender bias intruding.

Salary at all levels must be similarly equalized. Leadership training and opportunities must be developed and offered equally to women. The Association of American Medical Colleges (AAMC) since the 1970s has offered annual junior and, more recently, senior women faculty development seminars. Increasing numbers of schools have developed their own junior faculty development programs, support systems and offices. The AAMC's longstanding Women Liaison Officer (WLO) program has once more encouraged deans to appoint women representing their schools and hospitals to this network which meets annually at the AAMC meeting to identify problems and offer programs with solutions that can be taken back to schools and hospitals.

At each medical school and academic medical center hospital, the dean and chief administrators must ensure ongoing oversight that women in medicine are treated ethically and equitably. Early, repeated and ongoing outcome studies among women students, residents, faculty and those in practice continue to attest to the need for major attention to be paid to the creation and maintenance of safe and equitable climates for women in medicine. When women can take their rightful places along the continuum of education, teaching, research and practice opportunities, all patients and all medical systems are better served.

Mary Robinson, attorney and first woman non-figurehead president of the Republic of Ireland, in her October 1991 keynote lecture celebrating one hundred years of women at Brown University stated: "Above all, we can see now that the cause of women is inseparable from the cause of humanity itself. A society that is without the voice and vision of women is not less feminine. It is less human" (Robinson 1991). Without the voices and visions of women, the same could be said of medicine.

CHAPTER 2

Leveling the Playing Field:
A National Perspective on Sexism and
Professional Development in Medicine

❑

Janet Bickel

Introduction

While sports analogies are not typically women's metaphors of choice, it is hard to talk about professional success without them, and the "playing field" seems a particularly apt one for discussing differences in men and women's professional advancement. A well-tended field makes for a much fairer game than one littered with rocks and pitted with holes. I know a professor of pediatrics who discovered a lone tulip blooming amidst rubble in a construction site. She shows a slide of it to illustrate how many women professors feel about their achievements—it's been a lonely struggle.

This chapter begins with a look at the playing field from a "composite" junior woman medical school faculty member's point of view. I focus from this vantage point because: a) advancement challenges facing faculty are also common to but more complex than those facing practitioners, b) this group is large (women assistant professors now number over nine thousand) and exercises substantial influence as role models for both sexes of students, and c) I am most familiar with this group's dilemmas and needs. My expertise here derives primarily from interacting with the over twelve hundred women who have participated in one of the seminars for women faculty that I have organized over the past eight years and from discussions with women at over forty-five medical schools at which I have spoken on gender and faculty development subjects.

The multiple forms of sexism, including doublebinds that women more than men must reconcile in order to succeed, comprise one major category of "pits" on the playing field. Next are considered the "boulders" of structural inflexibilities and advancement requirements that look objective but that work against minorities of all types. The last third of the chapter recommends imple-

11

mentable changes, including providing skill development opportunities and more flexible options that would indeed help even out the field.

It is worth pointing out at the start that creating a forum at medical schools for any discussion of gender differences in professional advancement remains difficult. The first reaction of many men to any subject including the word women or gender is that "I'm in the wrong room," and they leave. Another common and confounding opinion is that the increasing number of women entering medicine is fixing any difficulties women may have had in the past. Some men balk at the mention of gender, saying that they are tired of or angry about, for instance, EEO requirements or making scheduling adjustments because of maternity leave. When the subject of "women in medicine" is raised, other men express frustration because they can't tell their favorite jokes anymore or have to be more careful about touching colleagues and students. Confusion is actually one of the more positive reactions because it suggests openness to change and questions, for instance, about how to do a better job of mentoring women.

Women's reactions to gender issues also tend to cover a broad and uncomfortable range, though if they have anger, it is likely related to feeling underpaid or at a competitive disadvantage in getting tenure. Because they may be labeled "whiners" or "troublemakers," comparatively few women, even tenured ones, draw the attention of powerful men to instances of gender bias. Women who have worked to improve the gender climate become frustrated by the inertia or fear of other women or by backlash, e.g., men's spreading rumors (after a long overdue salary adjustment) that women are now being overpaid.

This lack of a forum and of bridges between the sexes means that the reasons for the continuing paucity of women in leadership positions remain poorly understood. Though it does hint at the suffocating frustration of running into an invisible wall, the term glass ceiling is not helpful in understanding why more women are not advancing. "Ceiling" implies that the powers-that-be are deliberately "keeping a lid on" the numbers of women moving ahead. In reality, many deans and department chairs are quite concerned about the paucity of women candidates for top positions (Bickel 1994). But the reasons why more progress has not occurred are complex. One crucial point is that, because of traditional expectations about the proper role of women, our culture does more to encourage and support men's career ambitions. The concept of "cumulative advantages or disadvantages" is also useful for considering gender differences in career development. Some advantages, e.g., socioeconomic status, or disadvantages, e.g., a speech defect, are relatively gender-neutral. But as we proceed with our look at the playing field, it becomes clear that in general women face more accumulating disadvantages than men do, particularly with regard to gender stereotypes.

Sexism and Stereotypes

Last Christmas, a group calling itself the Barbie Liberation Organization exchanged voice boxes in a number of G.I. Joe and Barbie dolls. Hearing G.I. Joe with semi-automatic raised suggest "Let's plan our dream wedding" and Barbie roar "Attack! Vengeance is mine!" is funny but also instructive about the depth of our sexual stereotypes. Similarly, even so-called universal plots no longer work when the sex of the protagonists is changed, e.g., "a girl finds her womanhood by killing a bear" or "a young man puts his business success first and loses his masculinity, ending up a lonely eunuch" (Barreca 1991). Gender stereotypes may seem innocuous, but they actually interfere with the work of dismantling outworn concepts of "male" and "female" roles with, for instance, "healthy" development defined primarily in terms of "male" development (Bergman and Surrey 1993).

Women tend to experience sexism and stereotyping as delegitimizing forces in multiple subtle ways, many of which defy labels. Moreover, to a great extent sexism is in the eye of the beholder. One path through this forest is to look separately at cultural, institutional, and individual-level problems, however much these categories bleed into each other.

Stemming from the historical domination of men over women, cultural sexism refers to those common disparities that extend beyond and across institutions. For instance, corporate insiders list nearly twice as many success factors for women as for men, resulting in a series of doublebinds that women must reconcile in order to succeed: take risks, but be consistently outstanding; be tough, but don't be macho; be ambitious, but don't expect equal treatment; and take responsibility, but follow others' advice (Morrison et al. 1987). Another illustration of cultural sexism pertains to "comfort level," a major factor in selecting candidates for senior jobs (Korn/Ferry International 1993). So long as any culture's leadership continues to be dominantly male, women candidates may continue to be viewed as risky and penalized because they do not look or sound like the traditional CEO. Kanter's work is relevant here. She labeled a group as uniform when composed mainly of one social type and skewed when including twenty percent or less of individuals from another type, e.g., women (Kanter 1977). In skewed groups, not only do tokens lack clout, they also face numerous loyalty tests, and any discrepant characteristics receive undue attention.

Because of its global nature, cultural sexism may seem handle-less. But when an institution undertakes a study of the local gender environment, problems can be documented, assessed, and addressed. For instance, the University of Virginia School of Medicine accomplished an impressive self-study of the gender fairness of its medical education environment and found that women's perception of inequity greatly exceeded men's. Until these results were available, the administration had failed to recognize that sexism existed; recommendations from the resulting report are now being implemented (Hostler and Gressard 1993). Less comprehensive but worthwhile are examples from institutions that have conducted surveys of harassment. For instance, the University of Toronto School of Medicine's study of first and fourth year students found that over twice as many women as men experience sexual harassment during medical training and that women suffer more distress than the men from this form of abuse as well from verbal and physical abuse (Moscarello et al. 1994).

At the individual level, many women face lonely decisions about how to deal with a broad range of "microinequities"–from deliberate exploitation to unconscious slights. While some microinequities may look as harmless as a drop of water, as a persistent drip, they can wear a woman down, interfere with her work, and exact costly tolls on self-confidence and relationships (Lenhart and Evans 1991). Some slights are quite subtle; many of these fall into one of the following categories: condescending chivalry, supportive discouragement, friendly harassment, radiant devaluation, benevolent exploitation, subjective objectification, considerate domination, collegial exclusion (Benocraitis and Feagin 1986). For instance, *supportive discouragement*: A department chair advises a new faculty member: "You're such an excellent clinician and teacher, you belong on the clinical track" (without exploring with her research interests or the tenure track option). Or *radiant devaluation*: A surgery professor says to a medical student "you're much too pretty to become a surgeon." Or *friendly harassment*: A department chair phones a faculty member at home two weeks after delivery of a child and opens the conversation: "So I've caught you at home goofing off."

Such microinequities and mini-challenges cannot be corrected by policies or edicts. Women must get better at recognizing sarcasm as anger and at responding in ways that educate their colleagues without belittling them. And secure men must become more courageous in confronting their less secure peers about ways in which they demean women.

Who Made Up These Rules?

All medical schools have policies governing the appointment and promotion of faculty that are designed to ensure both that high academic standards are maintained and that institutional and faculty needs are met. In many crucial ways these policies function quite well, but the increasing numbers of women reveal two kinds of problems with them: their reliance on the "old boy's" network and their temporal inflexibility. To begin with the former, in medicine, as in the other professions and academic and research endeavors, the specialists within each specialized field determine what will be studied and who the new specialists will be. While peer review has many strengths, and rules for inclusion and advancement may look strictly objective, specialists do have the power to reject what does not suit them and can remain oblivious to the effect this exclusiveness may be having on non-tenured academics (Menand 1993). Moreover, specialists are not immune from putting their own needs and preferences above societal interests and tend to be slow to welcome individuals who are not like them, i.e., women and ethnic minorities (Kanter 1977).

Many women do not recognize that written guidelines represent the minimum of what must be accomplished. Who you know also matters tremendously. In hierarchical organizations success is closely linked to the informal system of relationships; and the closer one is to the top of an organization, the more commonly evaluations and rewards are determined by subjective criteria, and the more powerful the informal system is (Case 1990). Academic medicine, as the business world, is not a meritocracy: one advances via sponsorship. Without a mentor and a powerful and effectively utilized formal and informal network, a physician may contribute a lot to patient care and medical education but is unlikely to progress far.

In part because they devote so much energy to their families and because of their isolation within their institutions, many women do not build extensive professional networks. Isolation remains a problem especially in surgery and in all the subspecialties and at the upper echelons (there is an average of only sixteen women full professors per medical school, including basic scientists) (Bickel and Quinnie 1995). Women are also less likely than men to obtain mentors (Ragins and Sundstrom 1989) and also tend to underutilize such relationships. Given that mixed-sex mentoring relationships entail challenges that single-sex ones usually do not, this under-mentoring is not surprising. Some men understandably perceive that a close relationship with a woman at work may be misinterpreted, and they thus may be reluctant to mentor a woman or may be less forthcoming with female than with male protégés. Psychosexual insecurity can subconsciously get in the way as well: if a woman does not signal any sexual attraction, the man may feel personally rejected; on the other hand, if a woman does so signal, the man may suspect she's using her sex for professional gain (Bickel 1995). Thus, real or imagined sexual tensions can get in the way. Moreover, since women's developmental stages tend to be more complex and diverse than men's (Jeruchim and Shapiro 1992), many women are looking for a different model of the mentor relationship than can be provided by senior men who have limited experience with protégés with loyalties divided between career and family.

Without a solid network, a mentor and an understanding of the organizational culture derived from these, many women are slow to realize that hard work is usually not enough to ensure advancement. When they discover the importance of unwritten rules, including the "meeting before the meeting" and of knowing the decision-makers, some women conclude that life is too short for such one-upmanship and other similar games and stop trying to compete for tenure and other academic prizes. But even stellar women with enduring ambition report difficulties breaking into the existing network, either because they are purposely excluded, do not play golf, are not as active in professional societies or are too busy with the lateral functions of society, e.g., nurturing the development of others.

The other type of rule-related "boulder" in women's way is a set of synchronous clocks: their biological clock, their career clock, and often their partner's clock. The need to manage these clocks is a disadvantage in a setting designed for men whose lives are governed only by their own career clock. The current generation of deans and chairs have benefitted enormously from having full-time back-up at home to take care of all of the rest of life's activities. The model career trajectory that is still espoused actually represents the energies of two persons, but only one receives the credit. Now that 60% of women academic physicians are married to other physicians, "the old way of demanding single-minded dedication to medicine needs to be recast" (Fletcher and Fletcher 1993). Not only does the sanctity of the full-time ethos in medicine remain a barrier to the creation of flexible policies, but financial exigencies and pressures on faculty to bring in more income also present difficulties.

As it is, tenure and promotion policies are geared to a 60–70 hour week, heavily favoring individuals with few other responsibilities. Many medical schools have yet to develop specific policies for maternity leave that go beyond categorizing it as a form of disability leave and only eighteen percent have child care facilities (Grisso et al. 1991). A national study of part-time faculty in internal medicine found that almost half had developed the position themselves, and many reported a lack of fringe benefits and promotion options (Levinson et al. 1993). At most schools, tenure track faculty even temporarily choosing to reduce their hours beyond the allowed leave must drop off this track with little chance of reinstatement; however, most schools do now allow a year extension of the tenure probationary period for family reasons.

Accomplishing Change

Courageous leadership on the part of both sexes is necessary to bring men and women together to dismantle gender stereotypes and other barriers to teamwork. Grand rounds devoted to gender issues and to barriers to women's professional development difficulties are excellent forums because most faculty, residents, and students attend. A higher level of intervention is to require gender equity training sessions for all division heads, as Stanford University Medical Center has done. Many benefits accrue from women and men acquiring a better grasp of each other's relational context and working through impasses (Bergman and Surrey 1993).

Because of the complexity of the challenge, only a systems approach to change can address all the pitfalls and boulders illustrated in this chapter. For instance, a study on increasing the participation of women in physics found that the following factors are key: the commitment of the department chair, the presence of more than one senior woman faculty member, availability of day care, and a safe environment (Dresselhaus et al. 1994). Within academic medicine, the Department of Internal Medicine at Johns Hopkins University School of Medicine instituted a series of improvements based on responses to a departmental survey (Stobo et al. 1993). For instance, workshops on eradicating gender bias were held with small groups of faculty and all division directors, and an office of faculty and organizational development was established led by a trained professional. Since these efforts began in 1990, the number of women associate professors has increased from four to twenty-two.

Adding Skill Development Opportunities

As it is, most continuing medical education courses readily accessible to physicians focus on clinical skills and most faculty development opportunities offered by medical schools focus on teaching skills, leaving a vacuum with regard to career development, administrative and management skills opportunities tailored to the needs of academic medical faculty. In one sense, workshops to help women acquire such skills can be considered mentor replacement therapy, e.g., designing a personal career development agenda, negotiating for resources, self-presentation, building informal networks, writing for professional journals, procuring grants, building a research program, conflict management, and time management. AAMC's professional development seminars for junior and senior women faculty, devoted to the above and related areas, were the first of their kind and continue to be oversubscribed. Attendees, many of whom lack mentors, bring such thorny questions as: I accepted a job that should have been given to more than one person—what can I do now? How do I negotiate a fair salary when my chair attempts to intimidate me by saying my concern about money is tawdry and detracts from our academic mission? How do I say "no" to my boss when I feel he's taking advantage of me? In addition to a forum for gaining feedback on such dilemmas and to the skill-building workshops, AAMC's seminars also provide opportunities to discuss family-related concerns and to build a national network of colleagues.

Many medical schools with active women faculty organizations have begun offering targeted professional development workshops, in some cases modeled on AAMC's seminars and sometimes open to men as well as women faculty. Some women specialty organizations (e.g., the Women's Dermatologic

Society and Women in Emergency Medicine) and women's groups within mainstream organizations (e.g., the Women's Caucus of the Society of General Internal Medicine) also sponsor skill development opportunities geared especially to women. Certainly, these take a variety of forms in terms of goals, length, organization, site, and expense. And the assistance of a meetings coordinator or administrator is key in handling logistics. But the consensus is that such programs are worth the effort because they fill crucial gaps in the knowledge bases of women and put them in touch with sources of support they never knew existed.

Adding Flexibility

Science editor Donald Koshland has stated that "a biological clock that requires women to make a decision about a family in the same years that their commitment to research must be strongest makes pursuit of an academic career difficult. . . . Professional societies and academia have a responsibility to ease the burden on women during this critical period" (Koshland 1993). A recent survey of U.S. and Canadian medical schools found that 71 of the 140 provide for faculty who choose to work less than full-time but whose full professional effort is directed towards the institution (Froom and Bickel 1996). Of these, 32 have specific policies for "full professional effort" (FPE) faculty, and almost half of the 71 allow FPE faculty to be appointed to, or remain on, a tenure track. For instance, Yale University School of Medicine allows FPE tenure track faculty to extend the usual ten-year probationary period to thirteen years. The addition of such options builds the loyalty and enhances the retention of committed faculty, likely offsetting any associated costs. In fact, younger physicians now expect options to be in place that support rather than condemn family health (Franco et al. 1993).

Conclusion

Playing fields do not level out on their own, any more than prejudices simply disappear. In fact, power and stereotypes reinforce each other (Fiske 1993). Powerful people tend to be so attentionally overloaded that they do not attend to the powerless; likewise, dominant personalities tend to ignore information discrepant to their stereotypes. Thus, however many women physicians are now in practice, some department chairs are still operating under the assumptions that women don't mind working for less money and that they have fewer research interests and professional ambitions than men. When she inquired of her chair why her salary was lower than the men at her rank, one woman faculty member was told it was because she worked fewer hours to make time for her children; this woman had no children.

Stereotypes of any kind deny the right of individuals to be appraised positively on the basis of their unique traits. Thus in medicine, reducing reliance on stereotypes is a moral imperative because physicians have a duty to ensure that their own bias does not interfere with the best possible patient care nor with their responsibilities as mentors for junior faculty and as role models for both sexes of students (Bickel and Povar 1995). Because of the entrenchment of gender stereotypes, efforts to change these must take into account what motivates powerful people. In addition to lawsuits, other important influences on powerful people are their own self-concepts as fair-minded and careful, public accountability, fear of invalidity, and their own higher-ups (Fiske 1993).

Just as many women are not happy with society's assigning them the "lateral functions" of survival (e.g., child care), many men are not suited for society's projecting onto them the need to succeed and to win. Another unfortunate result of sex role differentiation is that individuals caught in one role have little knowledge of the experience of individuals in the other. And, as one realizes with the experience of snorkeling, from the surface one can guess little about the rich life underneath. Women greatly need opportunities to snorkel within existing organizational cultures, so that they can gain the familiarity necessary to be effective within them and so that men can expand their image of what a leader looks and sounds like. And, however advanced our society fancies itself, relational bridges between the sexes require conscious building, if not through formal efforts as at Stanford and Hopkins, then with CEOs establishing a climate of gender equity through their own examples and through zero tolerance of gender discrimination.

Change destabilizes society and organizations and, especially when resources are tight, may produce a we/they adversarial mindset. But from a global leadership perspective, diversity is a fact, not a problem. Certainly one of the primary challenges facing leaders now is to increase collaborations among diverse groups and to see difference as a strength and a resource (Mossberg 1993; Westberg and Jason 1996). In fact, chaos theory teaches us to see diversity as a necessity (Wheatley 1992). From this perspective, modification of policies to allow more flexibility and hence alternative career paths is a way to assure retention of half of the best talent and new ideas available. As organizations must increasingly maximize their human resources investment, it is to the *advantage* of medical centers to do whatever is possible to prevent their women physicians from wasting their talents and energies and from losing the strengths of the diversity they bring to the policy table and bedside. The more effective medical institutions can be in these efforts, the greater will be their own success in attracting the best staff and students, many of whom will be women.

CHAPTER 3

Women's Programs at Medical Schools and Feminism: What is the Intersection?

□

Delese Wear and Janet Bickel

Introduction

How do women medical educators relate to feminism? What kind of feminist presence is described by women in the medical academy? How do women in medicine enact their feminism? This chapter reports results of a survey and follow-up phone interviews designed to answer these questions.

In November 1993, the first author distributed a survey to all the medical-school appointed Women Liaison Officers (WLO) in the United States and Canada (N=212). AAMC established the WLO position in 1977, offering schools the option of appointing one or two individuals, suggesting that they be both well-connected within their institutions and interested in improving the environment for women students and faculty. The primary responsibilities of a WLO are to attend the AAMC annual meeting and to make available to others at her institution the information channeled to her throughout the year, including a WLO directory, women in medicine statistics, a quarterly newsletter, program announcements and resources on building programs for women in medicine.

The survey consisted of eight demographic questions (e.g., location, degree, age, career goals, etc.), while the remaining four questions focused on feminism. These latter questions sought to determine the following: if the respondent identified herself as feminist (yes/no); how she defined feminism (a forced choice with four definitions provided); if and how she enacted her commitments to women in medicine in the areas of teaching, research, and service (could check none or all of the examples provided in each area, including one open-ended "other"); and how she perceived the overall climate for women students, residents, and faculty at her institution (a forced choice with five descriptors). A final question determined if the respondent would agree to a follow-up telephone interview. Because a respondent would need to provide her name on the survey if she agreed to a telephone interview, the cover letter outlined how her anonymity would be preserved.

Results

Demographics

Fifty-seven percent of the surveys were returned (N=122). All respondents were faculty or administrators at North American medical schools (94% U.S., 6% Canada). The majority of respondents were M.D.s (79%), with the remaining Ph.D.s (16%) or other (5%); in the population of WLOs, 80% are M.D., 16% Ph.D., and 4% other. The range in respondents' age was 34 to 70, with a mean of 47 and standard deviation of 7.3. The number of years respondents had worked in an academic center ranged from 2 to 44 years, with a mean of 15 and standard deviation of 7.7. Information on the latter two variables is not available on the population of WLOs. Responses to the question on current job title(s) revealed that the following specialties were represented: pediatrics, family practice, medicine, surgery, radiology, pathology, obstetrics/gynecology, anesthesiology, neurology, psychiatry, microbiology, immunology, pharmacology, neurobiology, and anatomy. The following administrative positions were represented: directors and assistant/associate deans of student affairs, academic affairs, admissions, women, minority affairs, and medical education. All professorial ranks were represented.

Feminism

When asked, "Do you consider yourself a feminist?", 70% answered yes, 26% answered no, and 4% did not answer. The next item asked respondents to check which of the four descriptions of feminism best matched their definitions or perceptions.*

The item read: "In my opinion, feminism is an educational, social, and economic movement that (choose only one):

1. works through the legal system to improve the quality of women's lives; the intent is NOT TO DISSOLVE gender differences but to rid society of gender inequality;
2. works through the legal system to improve the quality of women's lives; the intent is TO DISSOLVE gender differences and to rid society of gender inequality;

---

*The multiple meanings of feminism made construction of discrete definitions difficult; there is much overlap between and among these definitions.

3. recognizes that women's oppression is tied to race, social class, and sexual orientation; feminist reform means reform in all these areas;

4. seeks to dismantle all patriarchal dimensions of society; celebrates gender differences; can be separatist.

Most respondents (60%) linked their perception of feminism to the first definition, what we here call classic "liberal" feminism. The second definition ("androgynous") was selected by 6% of respondents; 16%, the third definition ("multilayered"); 12%, the fourth definition ("radical"); 6% did not select a definition. While both self-identified feminists and nonfeminists selected the classic definition most frequently (68% and 41% respectively), 31% of nonfeminists selected the radical definition of feminism, compared to 6% of the feminists. Clearly some respondents' unwillingness to identify themselves as feminists stems from their perception of feminism as a separatist movement.

Enactment of commitment to women

Regardless of whether or not WLOs identify themselves as feminists, how do they enact their commitment to women in medicine? While their actions are undoubtedly more idiosyncratic and nuanced than these, we offered three areas WLOs could select indicating their commitment to improving the status of women.

Teaching

The five items under this area examined if and how WLOs: (1) ensure women's representation in curriculum materials, (2) ensure women's representation as lecturers; (3) systematically attempt to treat women students equally to men in terms of their (WLO's) verbal and nonverbal behaviors; (4) identify sexist biases in the content they teach; and (5) encourage students to identify sexist biases in their educational/clinical experiences. Respondents could check as many items as they wished, or none (not all respondents teach).

All items were checked more often than they were left blank. Given its comparative ease, it is not surprising that respondents selected item 3 most often (90%). Respondents checked item 5 least often, probably an indication of the difficulty of addressing sexist biases in educational/clinical experiences. Even at that, WLOs checked this item more often than they did not (53%). These responses suggest that via their teaching behaviors and curriculum development, WLOs are committed to improvements on behalf of women that will produce better doctors of both sexes.

Research

The five items in this category sought to discover if and how WLOs: 1) attempt to identify and correct the cumulative influence of male bias in their research, 2) do research for or about women, 3) engage in collaborative research with women 4) belong to women's professional organizations within their discipline, and 5) formally challenge sexism within their discipline (e.g., writing letters, review articles, peer review of proposals or manuscripts, etc.). Since fewer WLOs engage in research than in teaching, it is not surprising that the only item checked more often than not was number 4, indicating that the most prevalent enactment of WLOs' feminist commitment in their research was joining women's organizations within their discipline (60%). Only 18% reported confronting sexist practices in their disciplines via letters, reviews, etc.

Service

The four items here asked if WLOs 1) serve on committees within the medical community specifically charged with improving the quality of women's lives (as faculty, students, or patients), 2) bring to their other, general committee work the same agenda as item 1, 3) contribute time or expertise to projects that improve the quality of women's lives outside their workplace (women's shelters, women's health collectives, etc.), and 4) formally mentor women who are medical students, residents, or less experienced attending physicians.

WLOs overwhelmingly checked items 1, 2, and 4 (84%, 86%, 85%), indicating substantial commitment to improve women's lives *within* medicine. Probably because of competing priorities and lack of time, WLOs were less likely to be involved in community organizations to improve women's lives (40%). It is also possible, however, that some of these women view community-based advocacy groups or centers as too polemic. In the phone interviews, it became clear that even for self-identified feminists, some of the goals now associated with feminism are well out of their range of beliefs and concerns.

Interviews

In this account of WLOs' beliefs about feminism, we wanted to include their voices and some of their stories. Thirty of the 102 WLOs who had indicated on their surveys that they would be willing to participate in a follow-up telephone interview were randomly selected. Primarily due to scheduling, the first author ultimately interviewed only 18 women. Of these 18, 16 had indicated on the survey that they were feminists, one was not, and one wrote that she "avoided all labels."

The first question asked respondents to elaborate on feminism: "What are your conceptions (definition/beliefs) of feminism? Has the feminist movement influenced what you're doing with your life? In what ways?" The second set of questions asked respondents to elaborate on their answer to the survey item regarding the climate for women at their institution.

Feminism and its influence on WLOs

One WLO perceived feminism as a movement that "advocates the same rights for women as those granted to men . . . it is political and economic." According to another, feminism represents "a major shift in the mindset of society . . . [it is] an attempt to rearrange thinking about women in society, [asking] women and men to look differently at what women do." This way of looking at feminism is shared by most of those interviewed, reflecting the 60% of the surveyed WLOs who selected the classic liberal conception of feminism. That none of the interviewed WLOs raised issues related to sexual orientation, race, and class probably reflects their lack of awareness or involvement in current feminist theorizing.

In their answers regarding how feminism had influenced them, WLOs' answers centered around "confidence" and the continuing challenges in their immediate situations pertaining to achieving equity.

Confidence

Most often respondents reflected on how the feminist movement had given them a greater belief in themselves or reinforced confidence they already had regarding what they could do with their lives. "I realized I could do anything I wanted . . . even apply to medical school," one WLO reflected. Another came to realize that she didn't *have* to do "conventional" things with her life; another believed the movement dismantled "predefined expectations for women . . . opening the possibility of defining ourselves." Several WLOs cited feminists as role models who "opened my eyes," who "changed my attitudes about my own abilities." One responded that because she grew up with feminism, "I assumed I'd have a career . . . [it wasn't] *whether* I'd have a career, but *what* career." Another believed that the feminist movement had a "profound" effect on her life by "recasting women's roles" when she was at a point of making career choices. Or, as one respondent put it: "It's why I'm a doctor, not a nurse. " Likewise, one respondent related that she was told early in her life that she "liked to give the orders, not take them." This woman called feminism "fundamental" in its influence on her decision to be a doctor and on whom she married.

Several WLOs (even those who identified themselves as feminists) noted problems with the feminist movement, such as "the pitch is too high" and "the goals too directed . . . [which can] isolate women and even have an adverse effect on some women." Several believed organized feminism such as the National Organization of Women and other similar groups have "stepped too far by aligning themselves with man-hating." Such negative perceptions are indeed common in society. Given these problematic perceptions and the immediate challenges of their work and home lives, it is not surprising that WLOs did not voice contemporary feminist concerns about the earlier movement's exclusive focus on white, educated, heterosexual, western women.

Equity

Those interviewed indicated inequities between men and women in the areas of parenting and institutional power (i.e., pay, promotions, and status). One WLO who had cited a positive influence of the feminist movement in her life stated: "We were propelled into a situation we didn't fully understand. . . . We signed up for many jobs, unaware of the difficulties in integrating them all. . . . Somebody *still* has to have the babies . . . and somebody has to care for those babies, and *care about* those who care for those babies." Another WLO similarly noted the seeming dichotomy for women to have a "full family life and a full work life," especially when the workplace "ignores the reality of [many women's] lives."

With regard to power, nine of the eighteen women interviewed described institutions that had few or no women serving as department chairs, associate deans, or in key positions on powerful committees. One WLO characterized it as "a vicious cycle: if you're not on the right committees, if you're not accruing the right points, you're not seen as a potential leader." Instead, she noted, women are well represented in "labor intensive" but hidden administrative positions or committees. The reasons behind the remaining equity gaps mentioned by WLOs range from overt sexist practices, to ignorance on the part of decision-makers, to the choices of women themselves. Pay equity arose several times during the interviews, with views ranging from "clear discrimination" to "it's difficult to untangle because of the variety of sources of salaries." One WLO described a "salary equity analysis" at her institution that revealed clear gender bias in salaries that were remedied.

Overall climate

The second part of the interview asked respondents to elaborate on their answer to the item: "The overall climate for women (students, residents, faculty) at my college is (a) hostile (b) detached (c) impartial (d) encouraging (e) nurturing." Of those WLOs who responded, 5 (4%) classified their environment as hostile, 31 (25%) as detached, 27 (22%) as impartial, 42 (34%) as encouraging, and 7 (6%) as nurturing (sd=1.035). Of those interviewed, 2 (11%) characterized their environment as hostile, 4 (22%) as detached, 4 (22%) as impartial, 5 (27%) as encouraging, and 2 (11%) as nurturing, while one was unable to characterize her environment. Naturally, WLOs who traffic back and forth between hospital settings, private offices, and medical schools that are geographically distinct found this question difficult to answer.

What made their environment *hostile*, according to the two who labeled it so, were attitudes ("women are not perceived to be as serious about their work as men are") and institutionalized sexism. For instance, one observed that the whole "ethos of the medical center" is antithetical to the integration of doctoring and parenting.

The four WLOs who selected *detached* did describe environments neither overtly hostile nor noticeably nurturing, characterized by ambiguity and aloofness, peopled by those who were more "unaware" than insensitive. For example, one noted that her institution had large numbers of women residents in surgery, but had "no women chairs and few women division heads." Another remarked "there is no *active* support of women. . . . The system can eat you up." A third respondent characterized her environment as conservative and without malice; she believed that most people in her institution would acknowledge the concerns of women in medicine, but "nobody has the time to do anything." A fourth WLO spoke of the dean as someone who "perceived himself as a supporter of women" but "doesn't initiate anything on his own" and "makes remarks that he doesn't know are inappropriate."

With regard to impartial environments, checked by four of the WLOs interviewed, one respondent viewed her WLO appointment as the dean's way of legitimizing women's concerns. Similarly, another called her dean "openly pro-woman" but noted his lack of influence on department chairs' attitudes. Thus, while her institution is "impartial on a formal basis, it is a far cry from what it could be."

The five WLOs who described their environment as *encouraging* commented: "everybody is trying," "people do take women more seriously now," and "administrators do not ascribe to old-boy networks." One WLO noted high representation of women in all disciplines except surgery and described residency programs where pregnancy and family issues are "worked out" to meet the needs of women. Another used the word "empowered" to describe women in her setting, tracing this outlook back to the national "hullabaloo surrounding sexual harassment" (i.e., the Thomas-Hill hearings).

Nurturing environments, indicated by two WLOs, were established in part with "leadership from the top." Such leadership may not necessarily be reflected in rules and formal policies but is evident in the "unwritten ethos" of the institution. One WLO described her setting as a "community of professionals oriented toward taking care of all people . . . with less bureaucracy." This common standard of care for patients, she maintained, translates directly into how caregivers treat each other.

Discussion and Conclusion

We studied WLOs because by virtue of their appointments, they should be interested in and informed about the status and concerns of women in their institutions. We sought insights into how the goals of feminism are perceived and enacted by these essential women. Given the conservatism of the medical academy and the controversy and misperceptions that haunt the feminist label, we were gratified to learn that 70% of WLOs identify themselves feminist. We were not surprised that fewer than a third of these identify with the more contemporary and radical brands of feminism. Most are fully engaged in teaching medical students, providing health care, and conducting research, and thus are enacting what they hope feminism will help achieve: furthering the physical, emotional, and spiritual well-being of *all* people.

What do these results say about the work that remains? Medical education and hospitals are hierarchical divisions of labor and power. Since the particularities of women's lives *outside* medicine played no role in the establishment of these systems and since few adaptations to ease the integration of work and family have been accomplished, this integration continues to be a daily challenge for many. But all the inequities that persist—in salaries and in power—have multiple causes and roots beyond the scope of this chapter and of any one WLO to combat.

Let us focus here on how WLOs can approach the work of change and take the lead in asking the most critical questions. These women remind us that much education still needs to occur. The neglect, verbal slights, and exclusion are often not calculated but rather the result of *powerholders' taking for granted their own profound advantages as a majority group with caretakers at home.* The task of explaining how uneven the playing field is falling to women leaders. How can they best accomplish this education?

In a conservative environment, a reputation as a feminist might impair a woman's effectiveness as a bridge-builder between the sexes and as an educator. The perspectives of the one interviewee who did not identify herself as a feminist are relevant here. As a high-ranking administrator, she sees herself as part of the establishment, while viewing feminists as those who are "attacking the establishment." She reported that she gets to hear a lot of different sides, is often asked to deliver messages to the dean and plays a "pivotal role as an advocate for women students and faculty and as a mediator." In these roles, she finds her non-confrontational tactics to be effective. Whatever labels this person applies to herself or to feminism, some would say that she is working in the feminist vineyard. The point here is that the choice of styles and strategies should be driven by the practicalities of the situation. Leaders and change-agents must size up organizational cultures and craft their plans accordingly.

One promising avenue is to approach equity issues as not just women's concerns, but as one WLO noted, "underdog" issues that "many will benefit from progress on." Continually considering how programs designed for women can improve the environment for everyone not only builds allies but also can facilitate obtaining funding. This strategy does involve a risk of loss of focus. For instance, Harvard's Office for Academic Careers was created primarily to meet the needs of minority and women faculty but its name was chosen with an eye toward gaining broad support. This strategy has worked well with one exception: some seminars sponsored by the Office are well enough attended by men that a sense of intimacy and opportunities for women to focus on each other's concerns are lost. On the other hand, communications improve with the men who attend.

The sad reality remains that women in academic medicine risk being labeled "troublemakers" and may even damage their careers if they organize women to work for change or focus on gender bias. In publishing resources on building stronger women's programs (Bickel 1993) and in sponsoring seminars designed to increase the number of women leaders, AAMC helps WLOs to overcome the stigmas and barriers to change. But progress requires the leadership of senior administrators and the readiness of male faculty to examine their gender stereotypes and to help level the playing field. All stereotypes are limiting and dehumanizing. Any successful efforts to eliminate bias will help to humanize the environment for both sexes and will mean more empathic care-giving to all patients (Bickel 1994).

PART II

Training and Workplace Perspectives

CHAPTER 4

Lighting Candles, Making Sparks, and Remembering Not To Forget

❏

Jacalyn Duffin

Introduction

When I began medical school at the University of Toronto in 1968, I was with the last year of the old premedical course. As had been tradition for some time, the first-year "girls" (as we were called at that time and without vexation) were invited by the Toronto chapter of the Canadian Federation of Medical Women to an elegant dinner with the "girls" of the graduating class. The guest speaker was a woman lawyer, who told us that if things were tough for women in medicine, they were infinitely tougher for women in law. We felt some pride in the achievements of the nearly six hundred women doctors who had preceded us. The dinner closed with a solemn moment in which the graduates lit the candles of the entering students with burning candles of their own.

We were profoundly moved by the dinner and fully expected that six years later someone would convoke us to perform the same rite for our younger sisters. But I did not attend the 1974 dinner, and I doubt that it took place. My friends and classmates did not speak of it, nor did anyone complain about its lack. It simply went away. In the intervening years, the tender memory of the evening in 1968 has all but vanished.

Feminism did not have much meaning for us back in the class of 1974. We were going to be doctors, generic doctors, not adjectivally hyphenated women-doctors but plain vanilla physicians—as good as, and comfortable with the men. Most professors were courteous and our male classmates were wonderful. They treated us as equals and voted for us in student elections; yet

I thank Roberta Hamilton, Lynn Kirkwood, Meryn Stuart, and the reunion of the class of 1974 for their comments on earlier versions of this paper.

many of them still paid for coffee and opened doors. One in particular—my dissecting partner who is now a cardiovascular surgeon in Peoria, Illinois—always made a special point to walk on the outside of the sidewalk. We knew there had been troubles in the past; some professors spoke of barriers and quotas on women students and interns. But we did not think feminism was needed any more; it struck us as outmoded whining and an unfair deal for men. Once in a while a feisty older woman physician would tell us not to let the "boys" treat us badly, and we would laugh about her seemingly anachronistic comments, as if they emerged from the mouth of some strange interplanetary traveller lost in both time and space.

We were naive. While I may be a member of the Toronto medical class of 1974, a hematologist, an internist, a historian with an interest in epistemology, a mother, a fan of Robertson Davies, fond of Handel, and partial to French cheese and wine, the thing that strikes people first is that I am a woman—something I share with more than fifty percent of the population; something over which I had little if any control; something that required no choice or effort; something that is not an achievement. It came as a surprise to discover that others perceive us as women first, before they see us as anything else.

The following account of my own peregrinations since 1974 is about how I learned (among many other things) to be comfortable calling myself a feminist. It is also about how I came to realize that feminism is a perspective that recognizes the *possibility* of discrimination on the basis of factors other than ability; factors that may include gender, race, religion, sexual orientation, and privilege of birth. These lessons did not become apparent until I became a full-time member of an academic medical center, but getting there was part of the education.

By the early 1980s, I was living in Thunder Bay in northern Ontario, where I had the only hematology practice between Ottawa and Winnipeg. I had married during residency and my spouse was now the town nephrologist; we were young, newly installed, potential pillars of the community; we had a child. My being a woman was if anything an asset, and certainly not a problem. Everything changed following the sudden death of my husband in a traffic accident. For a time I remained in the supportive community, but decided to leave the job I liked very much to marry again. My new husband was a Canadian diplomat on the first of a four-year posting to France. In Paris, I was hoping to do research and managed to find several possibilities, but was unable to formally engage in medical work because the spouses of diplomats were not eligible for work permits in France. Women diplomats seemed mostly not to be married; for the first time in my life, I had encountered a barrier because of my sex.

I was happy in France, but at first I was also lost and confused. My son went off to school where he quickly learned to speak flawless French, my new husband went to work, while I went to museums until I couldn't stand it any longer. I kept trying to find medical jobs, took on some scientific translating and a part-time position reading immigration files in the Embassy; but it gradually appeared that work in hematology would be impossible.

I began to look for something else. Standing in a phone booth on a tree-lined street in the 13th district following a disappointing interview, I suddenly had the idea to study medical history. I don't know why. It was a topic that had always interested me, but we had had little exposure in the class of 1974. I began looking for instructors in the medical schools but finally found an advisor in the Philosophy department of the Sorbonne. The distinguished physician-historian, Mirko Grmek, received me in a splendid Renaissance library behind the Bibliothèque Nationale. He lamented my inexperience and the paucity of my languages, but agreed to let me study. Because of my experience as an internist, he suggested I embark on an epistemological analysis of the clinical papers of René Laennec (1781-1826), physician-inventor of the stethoscope. I protested that I wanted to learn all of history not just a tiny portion; he explained, "En France, il faut avoir un sujet." In deep exploration of that subject, I would become familiar with all of history. He also encouraged me to enroll in the seminar of the great historian of biology and "normalien," Jacques Roger. Back at home on that first evening, I found a dictionary definition of "epistemology," a mysterious word that, despite its sound, had nothing to do with "episiotomy." How could I make such a study when I was not even too sure what it was?

Grmek and Roger were my mentors. In the beginning, they did not waste a great deal of time with me outside of class, but they tolerated my naïveté, responded immediately to my amateurish writings, and respected my ideas. I was quickly hooked on history and on my "sujet." The years of study passed quickly. During the public defense of my thesis, I kept having a wild urge to crow with laughter: if only my medical colleagues in Thunder Bay could see me sitting there arguing about the implications of vitalism in post-Revolutionary France. I was granted a doctorate only days before our departure for Ottawa, where my spouse was next posted and where I hoped to return to hematology.

I had worked part-time as a physician in the Canadian embassy, but felt a bit out of touch and was wary of going back to clinical medicine. I had tried to prepare the way for the re-entry by letter and by personal visits during a brief trip more than a year in advance of my return. Ottawa hematologists were not keen to meet me and few answered my letters. One, who eventually became a very good friend, ignored all my calls; another had his secretary telephone to say "Dr. So-and-So has consented to see you on Saturday at 7 a.m." I realized that however eager *I* was to establish collegial relationships with these people who shared with me the nine years of training needed to be a blood specialist, *they* did not view me as an equal, or a colleague.

Their hesitation was entirely understandable. Few doctors arrive in a community without already having found a job. However, more stigmatizing than my lack of current standing in a Canadian institution was my new credential as a historian. Dr. So-and-So said he might be looking for help, but he needed someone who could do real "scientific" medicine: "wet-lab" bench work, he called it. A year later, he hired a clinical hematologist with no publications and no laboratory experience, fresh out of residency. I learned that for medical people, my humanities degree, which had taken years of work every bit as difficult as my residency, was worse than no degree at all—a non-credential, a matter for suspicion. By becoming a medical historian, I had inadvertently earned the mistrust of my medical colleagues. Not until many years later, when I had had an opportunity to observe the tendency of women to choose interdisciplinary research, would this problem strike me as a gender issue.

Because I could not immediately find work as a hematologist in the Ottawa area, I accepted a postdoctoral fellowship in history, began a new research project, and sent off parts of my thesis to journals. Rejection followed rejection. Once again, I was lucky and found a sympathetic colleague in historian Toby Gelfand, who patiently read my work and explained the criticisms of readers who accused me of being "internalist," "presentist," "Whiggish." The crash course in social history from an American perspective was useful and I soon learned how to present my ideas in a way that neither altered them nor gave offense. Rejections turned into acceptances and I began to attend the big medical history meetings, where I learned that the world was divided into the "docs" and the "real" historians. Where did I fit? A second lesson became clear as a corollary to the first: prior knowledge of my medical training made some (not all) historians view me with suspicion: a dabbling doctor, a rank amateur, with a bent for hagiography or an inability to be objective about my chosen field. Doctors distrusted my history credentials and historians distrusted my medical credentials; one degree made the other something to expiate.

Meanwhile, the hematologists in Ottawa gradually became friendlier, as I continued to attend rounds without saying anything stupid, and was willing to cover the ward when they all went to conferences in the United States. Under my care, nobody died who had not been expected to die. In 1988, after three years of quasi-probation, I was offered a staff position, which I declined, in order to accept the more exciting if less lucrative opportunity as historian of medicine at Queen's University in Kingston. The Queen's offer gave me freedom to try a new method of teaching; my diplomat spouse made it all possible by taking leave from his work. At the time of writing more than seven years later, he is still the only male foreign service officer in Canada to have taken unpaid leave for his spouse.

Academic Medical Center: Women in Medical History

If you were to divide segments of the population into groups based on their presumed interest in history, medical students would probably figure in the least interested category. Yet some of this apparent lack of interest may be an artifact of presentation. I had been contemplating an idea to "infiltrate" history into a medical school curriculum by organizing the structure on conceptual grounds that would integrate history with the traditional subjects. In other words, I planned a little history of anatomy during anatomy; history of pathology in pathology; history of obstetrics in obstetrics, and so on. I had two goals: the first was to demonstrate to the students that history was a research discipline; the second, to instill skepticism about the content and durability of everything else they were to be taught. I hoped ultimately to have one history question on every medical school exam (Duffin 1995).

The professors of anatomy and pathology were immediately receptive to the idea, and I was teaching about the history of these disciplines within my first term. Others did not understand the request and some were hostile. But invitations to participate in other courses eventually came my way. I had to work hard in order to be able to teach about the history of disciplines that had not been relevant to my prior research. Along with new reading on the history of pharmacology, physiology, and psychiatry, I was forced by my students to realize that I also needed to learn some women's history.

Students still keep reminding me that I am female and that feminism in medicine is not a dead issue. One young undergraduate science major in her senior year told me that I was the first woman instructor she had encountered in university. A football-playing future-surgeon who was contemplating marriage came to ask me if there was such a thing as feminism: he meant, "Was it justified?" The unmet needs of students in this direction somehow became my responsibility if only because others had abrogated it or were not challenged by students to take it up.

In my preparatory reading of the history of women in medicine, I learned that *no* woman had been allowed to study medicine in Canada until the 1880s; very few who had managed to obtain medical training elsewhere dared to practice here before that time. The early pioneers can be counted on the fingers of one hand: James Miranda Barry, Scottish-trained and an officer in the British Army Medical Corps who had spent her entire adult life disguised as a man; Emily Howard Stowe who trained at a homeopathic college for women in New York City and practiced in Toronto for thirteen years before she was granted a license in 1880; Jennie Trout, also of Toronto but a graduate of the Women's Medical College of Pennsylvania, whose financial donation was the impetus for the founding of the Medical College for Women in Kingston, Ontario, the first Canadian institution devoted to the professional education of women. I learned that Queen's University medical faculty, my present employer, did not open its doors to female students until 1945, and, while there have been several associate deans in medical faculty administration, there has never been a woman dean of a Canadian medical school (Morantz-Sanchez 1985; Hacker 1974;

Walsh 1977; Fryer 1992; Bonner 1992; Dodd and Gorham 1994).

I also learned that women doctors have been described as flagging feminists. Our earliest predecessors were committed suffragists and entered the profession on a wave of militant feminism, but we have tended to be silent and in some cases suspicious partners in the women's movement of the late twentieth century (Drachman 1976, 1986; Lorber 1984; Strong-Boag 1979; Gorham 1976). Women physicians began to turn away from pronounced feminism as they became successful practitioners: one commitment seems to have been increasingly incompatible with the other. In her study of early Canadian women doctors, Veronica Strong-Boag concluded that their feminism was "constrained" by their acceptance of limited roles in restricted practice (Strong-Boag 1979).

I recognized my class-of-1974 self in the description and felt angry and defensive. Thoughtful writers have almost forgiven us, by suggesting that it was difficult enough for a woman to make her way in a male-dominated profession; having been accepted as a full fledged doctor, the last thing she needed to do was behave in an ungrateful or unseemly manner that might be offensive to her colleagues and damaging to her status. The women in the class of 1974 were like a host of women physicians who preceded and followed them: they have striven to identify themselves first as undifferentiated doctors, and second as women. The "girls" who earned their MD degrees have been *re*ceived and *per*ceived as being just like the boys. We failed to contemplate that what it meant to be a "doctor" was a product of centuries of male definition.

I tell the stories of the earliest women doctors as part of the history of obstetrics session, raising the issue of the connection between history and the present. This session has been singularly instructive for the teacher, yet it has been criticized by one medical student for being "deliberately and manipulatively provocative [from a feminist perspective]" and by another for being "paternalistic and chauvinistic *in the extreme*." Since I strive for balance, both comments hurt; but, the second hurt more than the first. On several occasions, the history of obstetrics session has been team-taught with two members of nursing schools. We put students from medicine and from nursing in a single room. These students are constantly being told that they will be working as part of a "health care team," but they continue to be taught separately in a form of intellectual apartheid that crystallizes traditional misunderstanding and antagonism. If only to advertise what we were doing, we asked permission to hold the joint class from the deans of medicine and nursing. What should have been a banal situation felt a bit radical: the two groups of students had spent months in the parallel study of similar subjects in the same physical spaces; yet they were disarmingly shy with each other and their encounter in our class was like a tiny celebration. In November 1991, when our school of nursing hosted an international conference on "Nursing and Feminism: The Uneasy Relationship," I paid close attention.

My experiences in historical research have been similar to those in teaching, although it came as a shock to realize that fellow scholars would be just like my students: they noticed my femaleness before they noticed my work. It irritates me when colleagues assume that because I am a woman, I must do research on women doctors or on women patients. While I admire feminist theory, I do not "do" feminist theory nor do I "do" women's history. My publications have been primarily in the history of medical epistemology (once I finally figured out what it meant). Yet I have been asked frequently to review books on women in medicine, or to speak as an expert on women's topics. When I decline or suggest some*thing* or some*one* else instead, people are surprised if not bored or offended by my lack of commitment, and I feel that I have somehow let down the side.

The faculty have been supportive of my infiltrative history course and of my research, and have entrusted me with other tasks—tasks which like my reading of the history of medical women have consolidated my understanding about what it is to be a woman in a male-dominated faculty, in a male-dominated university—tasks that ultimately made me reconsider feminism and what it can contribute to my understanding of events in my own past and in my present.

Academic Medical Center: Women's Issues in Medical Curricula

The success of the infiltrative history program was probably the reason that the faculty asked me to chair the Horizontal Phase committee of the curriculum. The development of our new curriculum was overseen by the Undergraduate Medical Education committee, which subdivided its work into four phases: three of these followed chronological sequence of medical education; the fourth was the Horizontal Phase, which was to oversee integration of what has grown to be sixteen disciplines throughout the "new" curriculum. The disciplines include community health and epidemiology, critical appraisal, ethics, family medicine, geriatrics, growth and development, health law, information literacy, history, nursing, palliative care, psychosocial aspects of medicine, rehabilitation, and social science including medical anthropology. Most of these important disciplines had no time in the "old" curriculum, and there are few faculty experts in each. Representatives agreed that longitudinal, integrated teaching throughout the three phases of training (hence "Horizontal") might be more effective than a single concentrated burst. With its sixteen members, including both tenured and soft-funded individuals, the committee is large but it has worked well. Our concerns were myriad, but for the purpose of this essay, I will focus on gender issues. We were not the only group addressing this issue. For example, a major faculty task force spent months studying and making recommendations for administrative improvements in the approach to gender issues among students, staff, and faculty; similarly, the Problem-Based Learning group ensured that violence against women was included in the case studies.*

The makeup of the Horizontal Phase committee itself is relevant. Unlike most other committees in the medical school, it is dominated by women; as usual, many of the women members are in marginal employment situations with contract or term positions. All the student members have been women. Several men left after brief intervals to be replaced by women who have tended to stay. Three women members also quit the committee when they left the university: one to pursue a personal relationship; two because they were unhappy that their interdisciplinary research was not given appropriate recognition. All but one were replaced by other women. I am still the representative for medical history, but at the completion of my three-year term, I stepped down as chair and was replaced by a woman family physician.

Planning for the teaching of obstetrics and gynecology was the task of a separate subcommittee, but there was no special committee devoted to the teaching of women's issues in a broader sense. In the general plan to reduce the number of lectures, several of us noticed that components being sacrificed in the resultant cutbacks often had to do with women's health. The Horizontal Phase committee decided to be especially vigilant and studied all the educational objectives pertaining to gender issues emerging from our own committee and from the other phases, looking for areas of overlap and deficiency. As a physician whose entire education seemed geared to the 70 kg (white) man, I knew there was a problem, but I had no expertise to deal with it. The other committee members were equally non-expert.

Without a department and without a separate gender issues committee, the Horizontal Phase committee found or wrote 78 gender-sensitive educational objectives to be addressed in the undergraduate curriculum outside of the obstetrics and gynecology component. We compiled the objectives and circulated them to encourage discussion about their merits and deficiencies. We received useful feedback from a national conference on the "Medical Education in Women's Health," in March 1993, organized and hosted by Dr. Ruth Wilson, head of the Queen's department of Family Medicine. A few objectives were purged; some that appeared more than once because they emerged from several

---

* The latter initiative was in response to an in-house survey of students, which revealed that some felt harassed. Its results and subsequent reports were challenged by students themselves. Our experience and our response appears to have been similar to events in other institutions. See Thorne, S. 1992. Several Medical Schools Have Begun to Tackle Sexual Harassment Issue. *Canadian Medical Association Journal,* 147: 1567–1571; Van Wylick, R. and J. Kwon. 1993. Sexual Harassment at Medical Schools (letter). *Canadian Medical Association Journal* 148: 1120.

different disciplines allowed us to eliminate redundancy, encourage collaborative teaching, and make room for neglected topics.

The project to identify gender-issues objectives was an exercise of the Horizontal Phase committee as a whole. The ease of our relative success with the curriculum contrasts with that of the administrative task force report, which raised concerns about monitoring and was delayed. A separate committee devoted to the teaching of women's issues would have been less effective. It leaves the issue up to the willing few (unfortunately almost always another group of soft-funded women hired for some other task) and allows everyone else (almost always tenured men) to stop thinking about it. Such a model tends to loculate women; it can also lead to neglect of racially or culturally diverse topics because they become competitors for the same kind of attention and because the *extra* faculty expertise to address those concerns with yet another committee may be lacking.

Despite the successes of the Horizontal Phase committee, there remain difficulties in protecting our time or in having our input taken seriously (in all areas not only gender issues). A male clinician suggested that our disciplines were on the periphery of the old curriculum and struggling with the new because they are not represented at high levels in the faculty: in other words, we have no *department* for medical humanities and/or social science and no voice in establishing policy. But existing departments are somewhat anachronistic: consider what goes on in our large anatomy department—most of it is cell biology, having as much if not more to do with immunology and genetics than it does with the kind of anatomy we teach to our students. Whenever "anatomists" retire, they are replaced by other "anatomists." Yet there was a time when anatomy, pharmacology, pathology, immunology, and evidence-based medicine were not taught in medical schools let alone elevated to departmental status. Medicine opened its doors to these disciplines thereby changing the mandate of medical practice. How did *they* become part of medical faculties? Could jobs in the medical school somehow be liberated from departmental control? We have made little progress in creating a new department to match theirs, or in replacing an anatomist with a tenure-track ethicist or a cultural anthropologist. But we continue to try.

The Horizontal committee proceeded in a collaborative manner to deal with many other issues; yet, its process constantly served to remind me that I was a woman. For example, in the early days of the new curriculum, I bumped into the head of a department in a hallway; he suddenly ushered me into his office with two seemingly contradictory things in mind. First he didn't like my casual use of the term "soft science" to speak of my committee at in-house meetings. He admitted that it was conveniently brief, recognizable, and possibly amusing, but it was "pejorative" and I should be more assertive and professional about the serious nature of my task. Second, he objected to our plans to hold a specific session on the history and ethics of animal experimentation. In view of his rank, I tried to be suitably deferential and refrained from giving him a lesson on the advantages of co-opting one's enemies or on the disadvantages of hiding controversial issues from intelligent students. But I wondered if I had been male, would I have been treated in the same way, or if he had been a female, would he have chosen this approach? A feminist outlook helps me to understand the behavior of my avuncular colleagues.

When our medical school received a positive accreditation two years ago, the accomplishments of the Horizontal committee were praised. Given that most of the members were women, it is tempting to ask if our achievements have anything to do with feminism and its role as an agent of change in medicine. I think that the predominance of women in a single successful committee does not reflect a real commitment to change so much as it reflects an entrenched imbalance in the school. Our accomplishments may simply proclaim the efficiency of women, independent of feminism and related research: women tend to do interdisciplinary work; perhaps we are also better able to compromise and negotiate from long practice at being obliged to do so. Indeed the *dis*empowerment of women may have worked to our advantage: powerless people in insecure situations work harder in service because they are more vulnerable.

Academic Medical Center: Women's Service

For the past seven years, I have been a one-person operation, offering five courses in medicine and philosophy, in addition to tutoring for problem-based-learning and providing a small amount of clinical service. Due to the nature of the endowment that funds my chair, I am in a never-to-be tenured "soft money" job, which makes it difficult to refuse requests to serve. When I ask, "Why me?" I don't remember anyone actually answering, "Because you are a woman," but I believe that it is frequently the main reason. The academic community strives for gender equity or at least representation on all its committees, thus, an extraordinary burden is placed on the smaller percentage of women faculty. My experience seems typical of other women in my university.

In 1991, I served on thirteen different committees; most were not as interesting as the Horizontal Phase. Time for research and writing came out of time with my children. By 1992, I began to say "no," but it has its risks. When I declined to serve as secretary of another all-male faculty group, I was explicit that I had recently decided to take a "feminist" stance on requests for secretarial service: I would be president but not secretary. The remark was greeted with stony silence. I was not asked to preside, but there have been no serious repercussions from my becoming selective about service.

In 1993, I became Associate Dean of Undergraduate Studies and Admissions. Still without tenure, I was quite hesitant to accept this offer initially, but confess that I was enormously proud to have been recognized as someone who cares about students. I do not yet have statistics, but it seems that when women are invited to decanal positions in medical schools, it is to the undergraduate component first. Is it because the "motherly" care of the youngest members of the faculty lends itself to feminization more than do the jobs that pertain to the older postgraduates or the researchers? I became one of nine senior administrators in the medical school; all the rest are men, most have at least one degree from Queen's. They are non-sexist, supportive, interested, loyal, and have treated me very well. Nevertheless, I quickly discovered that the job itself, through no deliberate construction by any of my predecessors or colleagues, "felt" decidedly "male."

First, the office: a large, bright room with a window, which I would occupy only part time, and a desk strategically placed to face the door and over which I was to interrogate the nervous undergraduates. Second, the support staff, all women, who worked full-time, four or more to an office with no window, and who asked me how I liked my coffee and expressed utter amazement when I retrieved a student file by myself (apparently no associate dean had done so before). These women all seemed to have first names only, while continuing to believe my own first name is "Doctor," despite my corrections. Third, the meetings at 7:30 a.m. Finally, the students themselves who annoyingly continue to comment on my being female and therefore somehow "nicer," although all my predecessors were as concerned for their well-being as any person could be.

The critical stories of my year in deaning cannot yet be told in detail, because many are still unresolved. To summarize, I have seen harassment, both deliberate and unintentional, of women students by male professors, of women students by male students, of women students by their male partners, of male students by male students of different races or sexual orientation, of women students by other women, and of professors of both sexes by students of both sexes. I have seen repudiation of women's complaints by other women. I have heard female candidates for admission to our medical school complain about faculty interviewers who asked them what they thought they "as women" could bring to medicine. I have little power to deal with these problems except to listen sympathetically; in a couple of instances my attempts to be supportive have resulted in strong public retaliations against me from senior faculty with tenure in this university and elsewhere.

When I left for sabbatical in January 1995, I stepped down as associate dean. I gave my dean three pages of reasons, citing many factors emerging from the structure of the position itself, the soft-funded nature of my main job in history, and my personal situation; I reiterated my vulnerability due to lack of tenure. He was gracious and over lunch accepted my decision without arm-twisting; as we strolled back to the medical school, he mused that it may have been his mistake to appoint me associate dean while my children are still in school. Don't misunderstand; he is a caring person and was trying to accept responsibility, to share blame for the difficult year I had had. Should I have pointed out how many of the other senior administrators were parents too? Perhaps, but I did not. The maleness of our academic medical world is not the fault of individuals. It is the legacy of an ancient profession that until just over a century ago was comprised and constructed solely by men—it is the legacy of our society as a whole.

Conclusion: Are there solutions?

My first reaction to this question is to recommend patience. More than half our students are women who will gradually take up positions of influence where they will bring their own perspectives to bear, based on their own priorities. If these women have assimilated the class of 1974 perspective, then they may join in propping up a version of medicine skewed by its embedded male traditions. If that kind of medicine is their priority, then those of us older women doctors (feisty or not) must accept their choice, and not be too surprised if they find our cautions weird and anachronistic.

My second suggestion is to involve more women in positions of real power, and less in positions of service. In fact, women should fill positions in proportions that reflect their numbers in the academic community, no more and no less. If the university does not have enough women faculty to have a woman or two on every committee, then they might find a new incentive to hire more, or at least decide to relax rules about service committees either by allowing some to be made up entirely of men, or by abolishing others. Women should not be made to carry the extra burden of representing all other women, simply because they are women. In this context, I remain highly skeptical of the value of separate gender issues committees for curriculum or administration. We should aim to make *all* faculty aware of these issues—not just women faculty and certainly not separate committees.

Third, is to foster the appointment of scholars in the medical humanities and social science to real academic positions. Dedicated amateurs should continue to be involved, but they lack the expertise and the credibility to promote the issues of concern to women and people of different cultures or socioeconomic outlooks in curricula and academic communities. They also lack the wherewithal to conduct more research into these aspects of medical life; and it is clear that research is needed. Sometimes the humanists and social scientists are not welcomed in the medical school precisely because they are critical of existing structures. We must be wary of decisions that keep them disadvantaged in research and on the sidelines of administration and pedagogy.

Fourth, abolish all departments. All faculty must be members of the university at large. The structure of our institutions was generated at a time when men dominated the profession, which was conceived of as an agglomeration of certain sciences; although there was no explicit agenda to make departments anti-female, maleness and male assumptions are deeply embedded in their form. Furthermore, the boundaries of intellectual endeavor, as symbolized by departmental rubrics, can operate against any scholarship that seems to participate in more than one institutionally defined area; any work seems to be thin or inadequate when seen from only one perspective. In short, institutional structures generate entrenched intolerance to interdisciplinary study. The latent power of existing departments against women waxes when individual members choose to view interdisciplinary activity as a threat, all the while professing to value and understand its importance. Yet cutting edge scholarship should challenge existing structures both conceptual and intellectual. It is sad to realize that universities, which have been "frozen" into a very rigid shape by the 1990s recession may not be in a position to foster original research.

I have had some worries about writing this essay for publication. I am happy, I enjoy my students, I love the privilege of being a humanist in a medical school, and I do not want my male colleagues to think that I seethe inwardly about the stories I have recounted here, because I don't. All my debts in both medicine and history are to men—men who taught me freely and fairly and welcomed me into their professions without hesitation. In our faculty, gender issues are valid topics, dignified by open debate and discussion, and the vast majority of my medical colleagues do not discriminate against women. I am confident enough of their continued good will to dare to make my story public. Indeed, a reverse form of positive selection may take place as some of us are chosen for tasks, *because* we are female physicians and are therefore expected to be imbued with the "nicer" qualities stereotypically assigned to all women. That too is wrong. It constitutes a form of forgetting, which feminism should not, and history cannot, endorse. To remain silent about what I have observed would endorse forgetting.

So my final suggestion is to reinstate the candle-lighting dinner. Not for women only, but for all our students. To inspire them, yes; but mostly to raise their consciousness, to spark them to remember that *all* of medicine—its content, its structure, and its participants—has a past that was handed down by predecessors and shaped by the people who practiced it within the values of their time—a past that may not have allowed individuals like them to become doctors—and a future that is theirs to mold, but only for a time.

CHAPTER 5

A Feminist in the Medical Academy: An Idealistic Pragmatist Account

◻

Mary B. Mahowald

The second part of the above title is taken from my dissertation on the development of a pragmatic element in the idealism of the American philosopher Josiah Royce (Mahowald 1972); the first part of the title identifies the context in which that idealistic pragmatism has been practiced for the past dozen years. My feminist consciousness developed as I was earning tenure in a philosophy department in a liberal arts college; I took it with me when I moved to a medical school/hospital complex.

In this chapter I have three goals: (1) to explain the idealistic pragmatism that informs my thinking, (2) to identify the feminist consciousness that guides my acting, and (3) to provide examples of how I, as an idealistic, feminist pragmatist, survive, and to some extent, prosper in the medical academy.

An Idealistic Pragmatism

Idealism has both common and philosophical meanings; these are related but not identical. The common meaning is expressed in Webster's definition of idealism as "the practice of forming ideals or living under their influence" (Webster 1993). Philosophical meanings of idealism vary, but different versions generally involve the notion that ideas, including ideals, are real. There are dualistic idealists such as Plato, who deny that material entities are real, and there are monistic idealists such as Hegel, who view the material world as a partial manifestation of the Absolute Idea. Common and philosophical idealists share the views that ideals are real, and that immaterial elements of our lives are superior to sensible elements. Relationships such as love and friendship, for example, are real in themselves, regardless of how or whether they are expressed. Hostile and oppressive relationships are also real.

47

Josiah Royce defined an idea, whether general or specific, as a "state of mind, or complex of states, that, when present, is consciously viewed as the relatively completed embodiment and therefore already as the partial fulfillment of a purpose" (Royce 1959, 24–5). Although idealism is often seen as antithetical to pragmatism, Royce's definition includes the pragmatic concepts of embodiment and purpose. According to Charles S. Peirce, who introduced the term pragmatism into philosophical discourse, pragmatism, as a method of inquiry, culminates in belief as a plan of action. This definition of belief and Royce's definition of idea both involve an emphasis on future experience. Although Peirce and Dewey are not generally identified as idealists, they were both heavily influenced by Hegel. Dewey's definition of pragmatism as an extension of historical empiricism also reflects an emphasis on future experience.

In his critical history of American pragmatism, H.S. Thayer defines pragmatism as that philosophical doctrine that "emphasizes the practical character of reason and reality." Anticipating a question about the meaning of "practical," he thus clarifies its meaning:

> What pragmatism argues as 'the practical nature of thought and reality' is that, since existence is transitional, knowledge is one of the ways of effecting transitions of events, and the only reliable way of guiding them. (Thayer 1981, 425)

Implied in this understanding of "the practical" are its process-context ("existence is transitional") and its insistence on the future-directedness of knowledge (knowledge effects the transitions and guides events). The essentially empirical orientation of pragmatism thus involves a necessary reference to the future.

For most pragmatists, the emphasis on future experience involves a notion of community or social relatedness. In Peirce's writings, for example, community is the means through which individuals can overcome or reduce the limitation of their experience. It is illogical, he maintains, to be anti-social because the goal of science, to arrive at as full and accurate account of reality as possible, is thereby impeded. The social relatedness he and others advocate is not a mere mechanism for avoiding error, but a reality in its own right. Relationships, for the pragmatist, are neither abstract nor separable from action. This notion of relationships is idealistic as well.

The classical pragmatists attribute an objective status to the truth they wish to know. For James, truth is what works. This coincides with Peirce's definition of belief as a plan of action. Peirce uses the term "truth" more circumspectly, as that toward which our search for knowledge aims, the final goal of experience-based, indefinite inquiry undertaken by a community. Short of that goal, our collective beliefs or partial truths facilitate action that is more informed than action precipitated by beliefs formed by individuals in isolation from one another. While our decisions remain fallible, we "cut our losses" by resolving our doubts through examination of the consequences of alternative answers to unavoidable questions.

Pragmatism involves a critique of rationalism, i.e., the doctrine that reason alone is an adequate means of acquiring knowledge. James, for example, defines pragmatism as a way to settle metaphysical disputes by considering alternative, apparently contradictory methods of doing so. Using the image of a hotel corridor, he describes the pragmatist as walking down a hall of doors that open to different philosophical approaches—e.g., rationalism on one side, empiricism on the other; materialism on one side, idealism on the other; monism on one side, pluralism on the other. The pragmatist moves in and out of the different rooms to find whatever may contribute to answering a concrete question. For an idealistic pragmatist, the answer represents an approximation to some ideal. For an idealistic pragmatist feminist, the ideal pursued along the corridor of life is gender equality.

Pragmatism also critiques dualism, i.e., a doctrine that views mind and body as separable, with overall disregard for activities associated with the body as opposed to those associated with the mind. James, for example, describes the task of philosophy as "an individual's way of seeing and *feeling* the total push and pressure of the cosmos" (James 1965, 48, my italics). Peirce, despite his esteem for scientific method, exhibits crucial regard for the central role of instinct and feeling. "Instinct seldom errs," he says, "while reason goes wrong nearly half the time, if not more frequently" (Wiener 1966, 208). Dewey reconstructs philosophy by first attacking the assumption of western philosophy that reason is superior to and separable from other human faculties, and alone capable of providing answers to truly philosophical questions.

All three of these pragmatists exemplify a critique of what has been construed traditionally and stereotypically as masculine, i.e., an impersonal application of pure reason to the data of experience. All three, along with Royce, present a number of views regarded as distinctive of women, viz., emphases on particularity and detail in knowing, relatedness and concreteness in valuing, interdependence in relationships, and feeling and intuition as legitimate sources of understanding. There is thus a great deal in the tradition of American philosophy that illustrates a feminine rather than masculine orientation. This may have contributed to my development of a feminist consciousness.

A Feminist Consciousness

Like many people, I was not always a feminist. I grew up as socialized as others of my generation and socioeconomic class regarding sex roles and expectations. My father was a New York fire chief, my mother a homemaker with five children; my father was the boss, my mother long-suffering and compliant. My two older brothers played stickball in the street, while I learned to embroider on the front porch. Attending an all-girls' high school, I saw that girls can excel academically as well as athletically. While I never got into the athletic scene, I was class president and president of the Debate Club.

Like many women, my education and career were influenced less by choice than by adaptation to circumstances or others' decisions in my behalf. My college and graduate programs, for example, were determined mainly by whether I received scholarship support. Perhaps because neither of my parents had a college education, I was unaware of qualitative differences in institutions of higher learning. I thought a Ph.D. was an entry ticket into a professorial position regardless of the university that bestowed it; not until I was in the job market did I learn otherwise. Now I tell prospective graduate students that a degree from a prestigious school means that your qualifications are assumed and you may disprove that assumption when you get the job, whereas a degree from a non-prestigious institution means you have to prove yourself if you get the job (mainly through peer-reviewed publications). Since I have been in a medical school setting, I recognize another criterion of evaluation by one's peers: grant awards, particularly from the National Institutes of Health. In bioethics, there appears to be yet another consideration in hiring program directors: an individual's skill in promoting himself or his center, attracting media attention, and securing funding from benefactors.

I first noticed the sexism of academia during graduate school when the philosophy department chair attempted to persuade me to take a course from one of the two women in the department. He told me that the professor was a "first rate philosopher" because she thought "just like a man." At that point, I considered the comment slightly humorous. Not until my first years as an assistant professor was a feminist consciousness explicitly awakened. It was triggered by reading Simone de Beauvoir's *The Second Sex*, and the stereotypical sex-role expectations I experienced after my marriage. Changing my last name on legal documents was one such expectation. Another was the presumption that I would move to wherever my husband found a job. Within months after the birth of our first child, I attended a meeting of the newly formed Society for Women in Philosophy, where I found a number of kindred-spirited and supportive women with whom I have maintained contact ever since.

During my first pregnancy, I weighed the following options: to continue at the same institutional setting (where I believe I would have been promoted in due course); to resign from academic life until our children were in school; to teach part-time, write and publish scholarly work, while also doing the parenting thing. Of three full-time jobs (teaching, parenting, and research), I felt I had enough energy for two but wasn't sure about three. My choice was full-time parenting, half-time teaching and half-time research for the next five years, during which we "launched" two more children. Why didn't my best friend (I dislike the term husband) do the part-time thing while I kept working full-time? Perhaps I had been socialized into wanting to be the main parent. However, he had the better paying job, and I could do some of my research at home while his required laboratory work.

My feminist consciousness was deepened by the experience of how academia treats part-timers, many of whom are women caring for young children. Part-timers, I found, are generally regarded as "second class citizens" even when they are as well or better qualified, teach as much, and contribute more to the profession than their full-time counterparts. Although I had chosen this route, I had not anticipated the psychological burden it would entail to go from full-time faculty status to a status that was economically and emotionally equivalent to that of a graduate student.

A return to full-time status was occasioned by my employer's need to fill the temporary gap left by the department chair's leave of absence: I was already available, qualified, experienced, and inexpensive. Following two years as a visiting assistant professor, I was offered a tenure track appointment to replace the man who was appointed Associate Dean. Partly because I doubted I might obtain another full-time appointment, I accepted. Five years later, I was tenured with a unanimously favorable vote of my department. During those years, my teaching and publications had begun to reflect my growing interest in feminism and issues of special relevance to women.

As a graduate student I taught a course entitled Philosophy of Man, delighting in the opportunity it presented to use works from my favorite philosophers. Not until I was a faculty member did I come to realize that most of those philosophers had views about women that were inconsistent with their views about men or with a generic notion of human beings. This spurred me to gather the material that these philosophers had written about women, which was usually peripheral to their major writings, and publish an anthology of their writings on woman. Each section was introduced by a brief account of the author's overall philosophy and his or her view of human nature. I still consider this book a remedial text, propaedeutic to an examination of specific issues relevant to women.

A pertinent anecdote is associated with the preparation of the first edition of my *Philosophy of Woman* (1978). Having been asked to teach a course on The Concept of Woman at one institution, I was already committed to teaching two courses at another. I accepted the third course because I felt that teaching this material would help me prepare a better book. For one full semester, I traveled sixty miles in one direction to teach that course and seventy miles in another direction for the other two. Little did the students in the first course know that as we were attempting to clarify the concept of woman I was developing the reality. By the end of the course it was obvious that someone else had been attending. The veracity of the concept was attested a few weeks later through the birth of our second daughter.

Having daughters probably enhances one's sensitivity to sexism. But having sons can do that too. When our third child arrived, at least one person observed: "At last you got your boy." The comment was particularly irritating because we were not even trying for a third, let alone a boy. Despite what we have heard about the differences between boy and girl children, our unscientific sample belies the gender stereotype: our son talked earlier than his sisters, and was slower in developing motor skills. None of our children asked for Barbie dolls or guns; all three played with Legos, our second daughter more than the others. Because her behavior tends to be more aggressive and independent than the others, I have sometimes characterized her as our stereotypic boy. She was much more likely than our quiet and reserved older daughter or warm and gentle son to unnerve her teachers, who interpreted her questioning demeanor rather negatively. Had our son behaved similarly, I suspect he would hardly have caused a stir.

Did we condition our children to unstereotypic behaviors? We may have done so unintentionally. But like most parents, our intent was to help each child be whoever he or she is. For a number of years, we had a banner fastened to the door of our daughters' room; it said: "You are hereby invited to become whoever you are." Given the sex role socialization that prevails, parents may need to compensate for its pressures by encouraging non-stereotypic behaviors.

So much for the development of my feminist consciousness and efforts to apply it in our family setting. What is that consciousness? This question may best be answered by describing the feminism with which I identify. It begins with three premises that characterize diverse versions of feminism: (1) women's interests have long been subordinated to those of men, (2) this is wrong, and (3) we should societally and individually try to rectify this. The first premise, a factual claim, is easily supportable by historical and current data that I will not here repeat. To those who believe that sexism no longer exists, I can only ask that they review the documentation to which I refer at the end of this sentence (Sidel 1986; Okin 1989; Navarro 1975; Weaver 1978; Pearce 1978; McLanahan, Spencer and Watson 1989).

A defense of the second premise, a normative or evaluative claim, relies on a notion of social equality that is applicable to both sexes. If equality between the sexes is not a good to be promoted, then we ought not to regard the subordination of women's interests to men's as wrong. Note, however, that gender equality does not imply that we regard men and women as the same, any more than sameness is entailed by the belief that persons of different races, cultures, or socioeconomic status are socially equal.

The critique of gender inequality that feminism entails is not developed in classical American pragmatism or idealism. It does appear, however, in the writings of Jane Addams, who was closely associated with two American pragmatists, John Dewey and George Herbert Mead. Addams proposed that "cultural feminism," a natural nurturant orientation on the part of women, is crucial to the arrest of violence and hunger (Deegan 1988, 225). Nowadays this view is associated with an ethic of care. An explicit critique of social inequality also appears in the work of an African-American philosopher, Cornel West, who coined the term "prophetic pragmatism" as a label for the type of egalitarian criticalness that feminism involves (West 1989). Although gender equality defines an ideal that all feminists strive to achieve, those feminists who are idealistic pragmatists value partial achievement of the ideal, recognizing that full equality may be "an impossible dream."

Since pragmatists view theory as inseparable from action, they are even more supportive of the third premise of feminism, which defines feminism as a movement and feminists as activists. Feminism thus insists that concrete efforts be taken to alter the wrongness of sexism, that is, to promote gender justice or at least to reduce gender inequality. There are multiple ways in which individuals and organizations can fulfill this component of authentic feminism. One way is to raise our children (boys and girls alike) to recognize and challenge sexism, whether covert or overt, where it occurs. Given the gender stereotyping that surrounds them, in which conformity is likely to facilitate their social acceptance, this is no easy task. Feminists may also be activists by raising the consciousness of others through education, publication, and example. Contrary to those who believe that words alone are useless, the pen at times has been "mightier than the sword." Similarly, actions may be more communicative and convincing than mere words. Whatever the chosen means, feminists are only feminists to the extent that they live or act their commitment to gender justice.

In the Medical Academy

Moving to the medical academy in 1982 raised two sets of concerns, one about credibility and the other about integrity. Both derived from the differences between that setting and the academy of the liberal arts of which I had been a part for the previous thirteen years. Some of the differences I expected to see were the following:

1. The medical academy is a more patriarchal system than the humanities.
2. Medical academics tend to have a greater sense of their importance than other academics.
3. Clinicians tend to be activists rather than theoreticians.
4. Clinicians make more money and enjoy greater social prestige than other academics.
5. Medical academics tend to be more politically and socially conservative, i.e., less open to movements that challenge the status quo.

6. Medical education consists mainly of memorization during the first two years and endurance during the next two; postgraduate education in other areas focuses on development of research and critical thinking skills.

All of these expectations were fulfilled during the next fourteen years.

The following features of academic medicine have also been observed in the course of my experience:

1. Doctors greatly outnumber academic humanists and represent a great variety of dispositions and talents.
2. The bulk of patient care is provided by those who have not yet completed their training.
3. Dying patients are more likely to have their dying prolonged than they would in a non-academic setting.
4. Academic physicians work longer hours than other academic humanists and are less likely to work at home.
5. Academic physicians function more collaboratively than other academics.
6. Academic medicine places greater emphasis on, and provides means of achieving, ongoing education to a greater degree than this occurs in other academic areas.
7. Medicine is less supportive of personal and family needs than other academic settings.

Some of these features, e.g., 5 and 6, facilitated my transition to the medical academy; others, e.g., 4 and 7 added to the complexity of my life.

While looking forward to the challenge of the medical school/hospital complex, I knew that credibility would have to be earned. But the stereotype of the philosopher as one who lives in an ivory tower could only be dispelled by "putting my body where my mind was," i.e., through regular participation in rounds in critical care settings and endless interdisciplinary meetings. The pedagogy I learned to practice was a pedagogy of presence in which all of us were learners. Needless to say, this type of teaching/learning requires a great deal of time and energy that might otherwise be spent on one's own research and writing. I felt that my persistent clinical presence would help to develop an atmosphere of openness to ethics teaching and activities throughout the institution, which as yet had no ethics program. Fortunately, this occurred. After practicing a pedagogy of presence for the next five years I hoped that others would join the effort, allowing me more time for academic work. Unfortunately, this did not occur. By then, however, I had done well enough to be offered a tenured position at a great university with a first rate program in clinical ethics, where my academic as well as clinical efforts would be supported and rewarded.

The clinical context to which I redirected my professional commitment when I first moved to a hospital/medical setting is now commonly emphasized in the literature of bioethics. Involvement in that context is neglected by some bioethicists, i.e., those who spend most of their time in medical school offices rather than hospitals, traveling to meetings, giving talks, and writing articles. It seems clear, however, that ongoing experience of context is a crucial component of feminist and pragmatic ethics; positions developed apart from that context illustrate the fallacy of abstraction.

While immersion in context provides empirical grounding for critical reflection in the medical setting, it also entails possibilities for co-optation that a philosopher or ethicist needs to resist. Being an acknowledged feminist among non-feminists is an advantage in that regard because the hierarchical medical system is hardly inclined to support feminist views. At best, the system tolerates feminism as it does other challenges to the status quo as a sign of openness. Invitations from administrators to serve on various committees, programs, and conferences seem often to be driven by the desire to be perceived as unbiased and open, regardless of the reality. At the medical institution where I work, I am frequently the token woman, the token philosopher, and occasionally a token feminist. Having tokens is better than having no one who represents a different point of view, so long as the tokens have not been co-opted.

Avoidance of co-optation requires integrity, the other major concern I had on moving to a medical school/hospital complex. Leaving a regular philosophy department meant risking the loss of my philosophical integrity. However, having learned from Socrates that philosophy belongs in the "marketplace," I considered the marketplace of medicine a particularly needy setting for the point of view I might bring to it. The best way to maintain my philosophical integrity, I thought, was to keep in touch with my discipline by attending and participating in philosophical conferences and organizations, and by reading and publishing in philosophy journals. I did that, and still do. Similarly, on leaving the support of a Women's Studies program for an environment where the term feminism evokes hostility or defensiveness, it has been important to me to maintain contact with other feminists, to attend and participate in feminist conferences and organizations, and read and publish in feminist journals. Remaining both a feminist and a philosopher allows me to practice the prophetic pragmatism described by West.

In time I was able to see explicit correlations between clinical practice and themes that I had learned from the American philosophers, especially Royce and Peirce. Both men support the case-based method and collaborative model of decision-making commonly employed in health care. Peirce's concepts of belief and fallibilism and Royce's concepts of loyalty and interpretation provide relevant insights as well.

Royce's and Peirce's emphasis on experience as the origin and end of inquiry is easily recognizable in the casuistry of medicine. Real cases raise the questions whose answers, rightly or wrongly, are applied back to the same cases. Because health care is so complex and the expertise of different individuals is inevitably limited, the best answers are generally reached through the input of many individuals, i.e., through consultations. The community of inquirer/clinicians base their decision on consideration of the patient's future experience, as influenced by the selected treatment. Each decision is akin to Peirce's definition of belief as a plan of action, resolving or at least assuaging the doubt that prompted the inquiry. While error is reduced through a collaborative or consultative method, doctors know that their decisions or plans of action may not coincide with the true answer to their ongoing question "What is best for this patient?" Peirce articulated this realization in his definition of "fallibilism": "the doctrine that our knowledge is never absolute but always swims, as it were, in a continuum of uncertainty and of indeterminacy" (Hartshorne and Weiss 1974, 70).

Royce's concept of loyalty aptly describes the clinician's commitment to individual patients and to his or her profession. Loyalty to a cause, for Royce, entails an altruistic practical commitment to a good beyond oneself. The good beyond self to which the clinician is committed is the patient's health. The clinician seeks to empower the patient so that dependence on the health care system is no longer necessary. Royce's concept of interpretation, which originated in Peirce, is a method of mediation between perception and conception, and between individual selves and communities. The clinician mediates between the patient's perception of disease and medical concepts that are applicable to that perception. Some physicians also mediate between the health needs of individuals and community resources for addressing those needs. Interpretation describes a healing process in which patients are interpreters to caregivers of the signs of their own illness, and family members and caregivers all have different signs to interpret to one another.

Observing and exploring these connections between philosophers I have studied and my perceptions of medical education and practice has been an interpretive means of maintaining my philosophical integrity. Although I seldom make the connections as explicitly as above, I remain an idealistic pragmatist feminist in the medical academy by practicing what that means, and teaching and writing about it from time to time. To preserve equanimity, the practice involves some selectiveness. Noting and challenging every instance of sexism might totally consume my energy, and would probably be ineffective. As a pragmatist, I'm willing to accept partial successes as valid and important because, as James remarked, "there is no difference anywhere that doesn't make a difference everywhere" (James 1965, 45). I am unwilling to forfeit small victories while pursuing an unrealizable purist goal. What's worth doing, I believe, is worth doing less than perfectly.

There are times, however, when one's integrity demands the risk of irritating, sometimes even alienating, others. Consider the following:

Two candidates were considered for the same position. The dossier of one had not yet been obtained; I knew neither personally. The male candidate was described in letters of reference, cited during the discussion, as "modest and unassuming, the very qualities that make him a valued colleague and leader." Later, the female candidate was described by another faculty member (FM) as so gentle and nice a person that she probably wouldn't be a strong enough colleague.

Thinking that the contrast in the evaluations should be recognized, I asked: "Do you realize what we just did? For both candidates we used language that could be construed positively, yet in one case we interpreted the qualities mentioned as a sign of strength and in the other as a sign of weakness." Although I had not adverted to the gender difference in the two candidates, FM quickly responded with another question: "Are you calling me a sexist?" To which I answered: "I didn't say that; all I did was point out the discrepancy in our evaluations." He then explained, to the apparent satisfaction of the other men in the room, why the male candidate was clearly superior. Needless to say, the minutes of the meeting failed to reflect the discrepancy I had noted.

A feminist must also weigh the impact of her activism on others. Consider, for example, the following incident:

A fellow in the high risk obstetrics service became pregnant with her first child. At seven months gestation, she started contracting and was placed on medication and bedrest to avoid premature birth. During her time at home, she prepared the main part of a review paper for one of the attending physicians. Although she regretted being unable to do the "scut" work required of house officers and the other fellow in the program, her colleagues did not complain of having to fill the gap. Five weeks later, after tests showed adequate fetal lung maturity, she discontinued the medication and returned to work. Within a week she delivered a healthy infant. Two days later she brought the baby to the department, where I chatted briefly with her. "It's going to be hard," I commented, "to return to work after only six weeks with the baby." "Yes," she agreed, "but I have to. I asked Dr. X (the director of the fellowship) if I could take my vacation now so that I'd have more time with the baby, but he refused. He said: 'Pregnancy, after all, is elective.'"

I was astounded by the reported comment of this high-risk obstetrician and his immediate unwillingness to accede to an apparently reasonable request. However, I did not wish to compromise the fellow's relationship with the person on whom she relied for a crucial recommendation. Although she did not want me to discuss the situation with him or others in an identifying way, she was willing to have me write up the case, disguising its details, and send it to an ethics journal that would invite and publish comments. Since the journal has a broad circulation, I believe this was an effective means of raising other people's consciousness.

Examples of the struggle to maintain credibility and integrity in the medical academy could be multiplied. I am fortunate to have found or created opportunities to influence the system and achieve at least partial successes. For example, a clinical appointment in the Department of Obstetrics and Gynecology allows me to be involved with issues of women's health on a daily basis. Teaching reproductive ethics to the full medical school class and clinical ethics to the physicians in our clinical ethics fellowship enables me not only to reach them but also those they may teach or interact with in the future. My publications, presentations, funded projects, and organization of series and conferences on issues of particular relevance to women are additional means of maintaining my feminist identity and having some impact on others with regard to issues of gender justice.

Like women in academia generally, we are a minority in the medical academy as well. Our numerical minority is particularly acute and troubling at the topmost levels of power, income, and prestige. My own field of bioethics reflects the same white male dominance that is evident in other professions, yet one rarely sees self-consciousness about that dominance. Until and unless the people who occupy positions of dominance begin to listen to those who are not just like themselves, the imbalance is unlikely to change. For my part, I would rather live with the admitted and overt chauvinism of some than the unacknowledged covert sexism of others. With the former, there is an honesty that can be supportive; with the latter, it is sometimes fatal to be honest.

CHAPTER 6

Father Knows Best . . . ?

❏

Deborah L. Jones

Although the word "feminism" has been in common usage in the United States since the early part of the twentieth century, it is hardly a word that I grew up with. I come from a white, middle-class family that is firmly rooted in the traditions and assumptions associated with patriachy. It is somewhat ironic that it is from these roots that my own sense of feminism has developed.

My road to feminism (although I did not know it and would certainly not have recognized the word at the time) started on the day that my father came home and presented my two brothers with life insurance policies. There was no policy for me. My parents explained that when I got married I would have someone to take care of me but my brothers would be in positions of having to take care of their families, thus they needed life insurance policies. This discussion took place in the dining room of the house that we lived in until I was ten years old. I remember being dismayed but really did not understand enough about what was going on to raise questions or make any demands. I have never felt unloved or uncared for in the context of my family, so it was not long before the incident became part of the past and my life as a child went on.

This early encounter with the assumptions associated with patriarchy languished somewhere in the depths of my spirit but for most of my youth I assumed and reflected the conservative and traditional values that were around me. Fortunately, education was strongly valued in my family and I was provided with the same educational opportunities as my brothers. That is not to say that my family envisioned me as someone who would ultimately have a career outside of the home—my father was a chemist and my mother was a mathematician who taught until their first child was born and then became a homemaker. It was most likely assumed that I would go to college, perhaps work for a year or two, get married, have children, and the cycle would repeat. That would be the end of it.

I had the good fortune to attend a small, liberal arts college for women. The choice of a women's college was not made lightly. I had grown up in the shadow of two brothers (one of whom is my twin) and had been overshadowed by young men in general and my twin in particular throughout my secondary school years. I relished the opportunity to study and learn outside of the shadow of men and in the company of women, and was encouraged in this decision by the headmaster (yes, male) of the secondary school I attended. Little did I know at the time what a wonderfully supportive and empowering environment a women's college would be. Despite this background, when, in my late twenties, I announced my intention to go to graduate school, my mother encouraged me to go to Katherine Gibbs business school instead.

It was only with the passage of time and the accumulation of life experiences that I came to see that the traditional conservative values with which I grew up did not fit either what I was seeing in the world at large or what I wanted to do, and that my values needed clarification and redefinition. As I went through college and then to work in a large city, I learned a great deal by watching, listening, and interacting. And while it took me years to finger the life insurance incident described above as a catalyst for my feminism, I have never forgotten what it felt like to have been the object of a decision that was based solely on my biological sex, a variable over which I had no control. Nothing about me as a person had been relevant to that decision. I also came to understand that much of what I had "accomplished" in life had in fact been made possible by the opportunities afforded me on the basis of the color of my skin and/or my background. It is from these life experiences and realizations that I came to paint "feminism" with a broad brush.

Feminism is a word that defies definition. Formally, the definition is narrow. The dictionary on my office shelf defines feminism first as "a doctrine advocating for women the same rights granted men, as in political and economic status" and (second) "the movement supporting feminism" (*Webster* 1988, 471). If this is any guide, feminism is primarily thought about in terms of women. The narrowness (and I maintain inappropriateness) of these dictionary definitions becomes clear when one lays aside the emotionally and politically charged term "feminism" and tries to define "woman." If one tries to extend the definition beyond biological sex the definition of "woman" becomes sticky, for there simply is not a monolithic category "woman." Women are varied: they come in all different shapes, sizes, ages, and colors, with variable cultural backgrounds, economic levels, social classes, sexual desires, religions, cognitive styles, etc. These variables cannot and should not be partialed out of the equation that is "woman."

Bernstein and Cock (1994) decry the homogeneous category "woman" and the "imprecise way in which it has been used to hide real and unchanging inequalities of opportunity among different groups of women" (B2). Grant and Sleeter (1986) note that "a failure to consider the integration of race, social class, and gender leads at times to an oversimplification or inaccurate understanding of what occurs in schools, and therefore to inappropriate or simplistic prescriptions for educational equality" (197). The fusion and definition of womanhood with other variables is brought sharply into focus when one realizes that being a woman is not necessarily the primary source of oppression for a woman. For example, much of the history of feminism has been written from the perspective of white women; black women often identify racism as a larger problem than sexism (Moldow 1987; hooks 1984). Feminism as a commitment to overcome the oppression and suppression of women (hooks 1984) thus also becomes a commitment to overcome the oppression and suppression of women on any basis, be it social, cultural, racial, sexual, religious, etc. Feminism represents a challenge to traditional values and assumptions as well as a demand for change. In the broader context that I have described above, feminism comes down to the issue of power—who has it and who doesn't, the circumstances under which it is exercised, and the extent to which one is diminished by its exercise.

Let me briefly review patriarchy and its manifestation within the professions before I move on to more personal accounts of its continuing presence in medical education and to the concomitant challenges for feminism.

Power, and thus control, in our society is vested primarily in white men. This power is sustained by patriarchy, which is a "societal-wide system of gender relations of male dominance and female subordination" (Witz 1993, 11). Grosz (1993) maintains that women are oppressed in patriarchal societies via sexism ("the *unwarranted* differential treatment of the two sexes, to the benefit of one and at the expense of the other" [149]); in institutional structures that systematically position men in superior positions to women and value the masculine over the feminine; and in language itself (for example, the use of masculine terms such as "human" and "mankind" to describe both male and female). In patriarchal societies, the relationship between men and women is always hierarchical.

As in society at large, those with power in the professions historically have been white men. Androcentrism (a worldview that espouses the primacy of all things male) and patriarchy are deeply embedded in the history and structure of medicine and other professions. Witz identifies three ways in which patriarchy controls female labor: inclusionary, exclusionary, and segregationary.

> First, an *inclusionary* mode, sustained by means of the family system of labor as a form of 'internal contract' within sites of capitalist production, where the labor of women and children is under the control of the male head of household. Second, the *exclusionary* mode, where organized male workers collectively engage in attempts to preserve certain spheres of work together with privileged wage rates, justified by appeal to the ideology of the 'family wage,' for themselves and to prevent women from entering these male spheres of employment. Third, a *segregationary* mode where male and female occupations or jobs are demarcated by gender, thus creating a hierarchical gendered occupational order (1993, 29-30).

Because the inclusionary mode does not involve paid labor outside of the home, I will focus attention in the rest of this essay on patriarchal exclusionary and segregationary practices and how these are manifested in medicine and medical education. To do this, I will quote from a paper written by a second year medical student (Jones 1993). This paper was shared with me by a woman physician who has team taught with me a seminar for second year medical students that has carried titles ranging from "Women in Medicine" to "Gender Issues in Health Care." Regardless of the focus of content or structure of class time (from didactic to visiting professor to problem-based learning), the issues of patriarchy, androcentrism, and inequality of experiences rise to the top like cream in a bottle of milk (or like scum to the top of the pond, depending on your view). At several points throughout the seminar students write "reaction papers" in which they reflect on issues that have been raised. The paper quoted below was written based on an actual conversation among seven women second year medical students, with the excerpted quotations denoting transcription of an actual conversation. These young women unwittingly and succinctly have identified the legacy of patriarchy in medical education today. After each quotation, I will discuss the key issue(s) raised by these women in terms of both my personal experience in medical education and my observations of patriarchal practices in medical education.

"How do we feel? We feel ignored, unimportant, and invisible. We feel unsupported, like exceptions, afterthoughts. We feel beaten back, we feel as if our passion is being sapped from us. We are losing interest in standing up for our ideals and beliefs. We are lowering our standards of conduct and of how we expect to be treated."

Every time I read these words I find myself expelling an enormous sigh, for I, too, as a female faculty member and member of the dean's staff, have also felt ignored, unimportant, and invisible. A few examples may be helpful. I have been told that I could develop my office and the services that it provides but that there would be no additional resources to support this development. When I brought in external funding to support the development of nutrition education in the curriculum, the portion of my salary covered by the grant was dropped from the school budget. The direct but unstated implication was that this portion of my salary would henceforth be covered by soft monies, for which I would be responsible. I lobbied for years to have something done about our office space because there was (quite literally) no ventilation, just two old and frail window air conditioners to pull air in and baseboard heat for cooler weather. This space was never on the list for renovation or improvement.

These are important illustrations of why women in patriarchal systems may feel invisible, ignored, and unimportant. In androcentric and patriarchal societies in general and in medicine in particular, women are largely invisible

(Conley 1993; Mies 1983). The history of science and scientific research is primarily a history of white middle- and upper-class men, in large part because men have written the history books and recorded their own achievements. Male standards and values are the norm (Shyrock 1950; Sherwin 1992). It is no wonder that these students feel ignored, unimportant, and invisible. The reasons offered by the students in the conversation I am citing offer useful insights from their perspectives.

"The Spring before we arrived on campus, we all received a letter from the medical fraternities. After reading the benefits of cheap rent and interaction among students of all classes I became interested in joining. The last paragraph of the letter informs us that there is only one fraternity that admits women and that they have only four places open for the incoming women. This made me feel unwanted, left out. Perhaps the letter next year could explain the options for men and women more clearly before anyone misunderstands the situation. Perhaps there could be an opportunity for women medical students to have inexpensive housing and interclass interactions."

These women feel unwanted and left out because they are. They are being excluded from housing opportunities and social experiences that have been and continue to be traditionally male. Despite the fact that one fraternity accepts women, the language—fraternity—remains generalized to the masculine.

Since the process of medicine in the U. S. became formalized in the 1800s, its graduates have been, to a large extent, members of a fraternity. Women were actively excluded from medical education in a number of ways. The application of science to the field of lay healing brought about the demise of lay healing in general and midwifery especially, both of which were largely the domains of women (Scholten 1984; Riska and Wegar 1993). The rise of proprietary medical schools gave those with access to universities and medical schools (primarily men) increased knowledge, skills, and tools. The lay perception that medical school graduates were experts moved childbirth from the midwives to the M.D.s, that is, to men.

By excluding women from medical schools, those with the advanced knowledge and skills became the gatekeepers of the profession, defining the knowledge needed to participate (Riska and Wegar 1993). In the 1800s, those women who did receive the M.D. degree were barred from supervised postgraduate training experiences as well as the credentialing processes (Moldow 1987; Riska and Wegar 1993) and thus patients (Walsh 1984; Lorber 1984). Elizabeth Blackwell (Geneva [New York] College of Medicine, Class of 1849), despite her M.D., was excluded from the medical networks that assured success in practice: "I had no medical companionship . . . I was advised to form my own dispensary" (Lorber 1984, 19). This was the case for women M.D.s in both

Boston and Washington, D.C. in the mid- to late-1800s, where women physicians were forced to open and staff their own clinics, to form their own professional societies, and to publish their own journals.

The male fraternities still operating on medical campuses operate to exclude women. The issue of inexpensive housing is an issue of substance, particularly in a large city on the East Coast. Thus, these women are at a financial disadvantage by virtue of biological sex. To say that the medical fraternity is a tradition is to say that the tradition of patriarchy, the system for the oppression of women, is acceptable.

> *"The summer before we arrived on campus, I was filling out the health form for the Health service. When referring to the medical student, the form said only he. Please ask the student the following about his health. I felt ignored, invisible. Perhaps this oversight could be corrected so that future medical students will feel as if they belong on this campus."*

> *"The language of medicine excludes me. How many times do you hear a doctor say, 'I'll send you to a good G.I. man, he'll take care of you.' Where is the woman physician in that scenario? Our syllabus and books say 'no man to man transmission.' Gender neutrality would make everyone feel more comfortable. I feel excluded. Perhaps [the school] could adopt and support a Gender Neutral Language Policy like other medical schools."*

Language is a powerful indicator of values. The examples above are examples of visible sexism and of how patriarchal structures/institutions universalize the masculine (Grosz 1993); indeed "generic use of masculine terminology implies that the male is the norm in society" (Rosser 1990, 11). Language is thus a not-too-subtle and often purposeful form of exclusion and we should question whether the examples above are truly oversights, examples of "not thinking about it," or simply manifestations of lingering patriarchal values.

These students have limited exposure to medicine at this point. However, they will find the language problem to be widespread. I am reminded of two examples that illustrate the range of the problem. First would be the department chair who, on the first day of a first year course, invariably states that "the 70 kilogram male is the standard for medicine." The second example took place a few years ago when a senior administrator introducing the speaker at one of the more prestigious medical school lectureships referred to the "distinguished men" who had held the lectureship in previous years. When he sat down next to me, I asked if he hadn't meant "men and women." As I pointed to the name of a woman on the list of previous lecturers in the program, he winced and apologized. Now, this man is considered liberal among physicians within the field of medical education, openly concerned with issues of equity and equality for women and minorities. He would consider himself a feminist. Yet his language was exclusionary, steeped in the traditions of patriarchy. That a feminist at this level can slip up so visibly goes to show that it will take a great deal of serious and continual effort on everyone's part in medical education to bring about the substantive change that these students, and indeed all of us who consider ourselves to be feminists, want to see.

> *"I arrived on campus looking forward to meeting my big sister so I could get some advice about the safety of women around Philadelphia. I also wanted to discuss more sensitive issues of the climate for women on campus, like, is the sexual harassment policy made clear to the community. When I met my big sister, she was a big brother. I was happy, but disappointed. Perhaps in addition to the second year student choosing the gender of the 'Little Sib,' the incoming students could also choose the gender of their 'Big Sib' so that everyone is as comfortable and happy as possible."*

This student is raising the issue of networks, which are acknowledged to be crucial to physician career success (Moldow 1987; Lorber 1984; Walsh 1984). Networks speak of commonalities. Networks of women were crucial to the success of women physicians in the 1800s because women were often formally excluded from the medical associations and societies that provided male colleagues with consultation and referrals. Women M.D.s were forced to form their own societies not only to exchange scientific and professional information but also for purposes of companionship (Moldow 1987; Walsh 1984).

Historically, women were excluded from male networks because the increased competition for patients would result in lower incomes for male physicians. Women were admitted to medical schools in D.C. in times of financial distress, but when institutional funding became more secure they were once again excluded from matriculation. The practice of exclusion based on credentialism was ultimately a strategy for regulating the marketplace (Riska and Wegar 1993; Witz 1993).

Exclusion today takes a variety of forms at student and faculty levels. Women (at whatever level) are not offered the same level of patronage and mentoring that men typically receive; women students often complain about not being offered the same opportunities to work in labs, thus gaining the experience, publications, and later sponsorship of a faculty member. Young women faculty hesitate to go up for promotion despite their heavy involvement in clinical care and teaching and high research productivity if they perceive a lack of support from the division chief or department chair, because failure will mean having to start over again elsewhere. Yet the lack of support and lines that make up a network mean that they will not progress through the ranks. Their energy and skills will be used but not rewarded because, in the words of two of my colleagues, they are not "one of the boys."

Exclusion also takes place at the student level, as evidenced by a group of male students who recently petitioned to form a "men's club," in response to the institutional sanction of a local chapter of AMWA on campus. These young men do not realize that they are already members of a men's club and do not need a school-sanctioned club to reap the benefits of the system. This incident is a wonderful opportunity for feminism to be asserted on this campus, for the issue of patriarchy to be raised, and for an open and lively discussion of the historical forces that gave rise to AMWA and other women's medical societies. These issues need to be addressed openly and visibly by the administration, faculty, and students.

> *"Orientation included many speeches. . . . The next speech was delivered by a future professor. His message included the fact that the faculty was very supportive and willing to offer help to students whenever we needed it. To illustrate the point, he showed a slide of a woman (student) on the lap of a man in a white coat (professor). There were giggles from the audience. I felt objectified, I was offended. Perhaps in the future there will be community standards of conduct which will discourage the use of such unprofessional slides. I was thinking, 'Is this what being a doctor means? Laughing at jokes that demean you, at tasteless jokes which display women as things to be flirted with, not people to work with?'"*

> *"I was in class one day and a male professor wanted to tell a joke. He thought only the men in the group would appreciate it so he huddled them all around him, excluding me, the only woman in the area, and told them the joke. I felt excluded. I was excluded and caught off guard. Was I supposed to challenge the professor and make him tell me the joke? I did not know what to do and I felt like there was no one to get advice from about this type of treatment. Perhaps professors could be reminded to treat everyone equally and work against human nature which causes them to gravitate toward people like themselves."*

These passages raise a number of issues. First, gender is a social construction. In patriarchal institutions, women are assigned less powerful roles than men and that reinforce male superiority. Riska and Wegar (1993) remind us that in socialization theory "the socially acquired gender identity will result in an occupational choice that fits and supports the gender stereotype" (79). Thus, the legitimacy of women physicians is being undermined by more senior members of the profession who see women in clearly subordinate positions, not as colleagues or leaders. Historically, women in U.S. medicine have been relegated (segregated) to less prestigious positions, be it to nursing, midwifery, or technical positions.

A separate issue here is the perception on the part of a group (in this instance women) that they must adopt or internalize the values of the dominant group (in this instance men) to succeed (Tobias 1993). Unfortunately, we have all seen this happen. Many of the women that we can point to as having "succeeded" in medicine have adopted behaviors that "work," insensitive to many issues as they made their rise to the top. How often have we heard successful women physicians say, "If I could do it, they can, too," when discussing such issues as child care and maternity leave for students or residents?

It is bad enough that instances such as the above take place, but the institutional response often falls into traditional patterns. The slide shown at orientation was clearly inappropriate and offensive, but for years both the individual responsible for orientation (a woman physician) and the administration chose not to confront the professor who routinely showed the slide as part of his presentation. When I made an inquiry, I was told that there were formal mechanisms by which students could complain. The issue then becomes one of risk, and for these students the risk is real. Eventually, the problem was resolved by the professor's retirement, but without a position taken by the administration. How can we expect students to take risks that administrators won't? Without feminists in positions that can challenge the status quo (and be supported in their challenge), these types of problems will continue.

"As classes started, I realized that my colleagues and classmates did laugh at tasteless and degrading jokes. People were openly homophobic and sexist, intolerant of all those different from them. I felt disappointed. Perhaps orientation could include, in addition to a discussion of cultural diversity, a discussion of general sensitivity to differences among us. Perhaps topics of gender, sexual orientation, and race could all be recognized as important topics of constant dialogue in our community."

By virtue of its design, patriarchy is not sensitive to differences nor is it likely to be. Patriarchal structures were developed to assure the dominance of men, and as we review the history of medicine it becomes clear that medicine has been the domain primarily of white men. Until well into the twentieth century, racial and religious quotas affected men as well as women (Lorber 1993). Today, cultural, religious, racial, gender and sexual differences find low levels of tolerance or acceptance in institutions which are still structured to maintain patriarchal relationships.

It is therefore no surprise to find offices of minority and/or women's affairs with little visibility within the institution, physically and structurally located well out of sight and power, with few resources to draw upon, yet it is politically wise for medical schools to have such offices and to be able to point to a few activities that are sponsored by these offices. To find an office of minority and/or women's affairs that has the full support of the dean and/or president, is fully integrated into the life the university or medical school, is highly visible and effective, is unusual but critical to the development of nonthreatening, non-hostile environments for women and other minorities. It is important to recognize, however, that progress has been made in many ways in many medical schools (Bickel 1993). The Women in Medicine program of the Association of American Medical Colleges has been extremely effective in helping to develop programs and to disseminate information related to women in medicine, and indeed offers a number of strategies that have been and can be used on medical campuses to help bring equality of experience and outcome.

> *"When I went to the first AMWA meeting I felt comfortable discussing these first impressions of medical school and the women there said, 'Oh, we felt that way, too, but now it doesn't bother us as much, we are beginning to lower our standards, it's much easier that way.' I felt scared. I didn't want the institution of medicine to make me forget my ideals of tolerance and compassion. Perhaps medical education could include tolerance in its curriculum."*

Women have long been segregated within the boundaries of medicine because of their perceived capacity for compassion, first into nursing and later into more compassionate or "sex-appropriate" (Lorber 1984) medical fields such as pediatrics and general obstetrics as well as those requiring better interpersonal skills (Riska and Wegar 1993). It is consistent with patriarchy that the women holding associate or assistant dean positions in U.S. medical schools are most often assigned to student affairs, the office that is traditionally assigned duties of nurturing and caring for students.

> *"I started learning medicine, I loved what I was learning, but sometimes left class with unanswered questions. I have taken human anatomy and have never seen a picture of a girl's hymen; how will I know if a child has been sexually abused if I do not know what 'normal' is? I learned about the prevalence of hernias in women and have not seen a picture of a woman's inguinal region in an anatomy atlas."*

> *"Men's anatomy was presented as the standard with women's anatomy described only as 'the parallel structures.' Aren't all fetuses structurally female until testosterone is added to the system to induce changes? I felt invisible. I felt as if my body was not worth our time and energy. Half of my patients will be female; I want to have a strong base of information to apply to all my patients. Perhaps our curriculum could stress both men's and women's bodies and health."*

> *"We had a course in clinical medicine which included one-hour lectures on issues in medicine—smoking cessation, drug addition, and AIDS were among the topics. Also included was 'women's health'. One hour. Women's health is not just a topic in medicine, it is medicine. After that hour, I knew only that women are different from men. As a medical student, I realized my*

ignorance. As a woman, I felt as if doctors were being taught that my health was unimportant. It seems as if we are learning about men's health every day and spent one hour learning about our female patients. Perhaps we can learn about everyone's health."

"In a course called 'Life Cycle' we did not learn about the issues surrounding menstruation, PMS, or menopause. I felt cheated. I think it is important for me to learn about and discuss these life changes before I discuss them with my patients. Perhaps we as future doctors could learn about one of the most profound changes each of our female patients will be experiencing."

The examples cited above highlight the androcentrism that is still present in medicine today. Just as "white man is still the measure, the universal, the starting point" in academia (Bernstein and Cock 1994), so it is in medicine, where male standards are the norm against which theories are developed and tested (Sherwin 1992; Shyrock 1950). In medicine, things female are presented as deviations from things male. Certainly medical research has used the male as primary subject, extrapolating results to women. Men in medicine are the center of the world. This worldview goes hand in hand with patriarchy and contributes to the invisibility of women.

"I just learned from the dean about the school's Sexual Harassment Policy. My friends did not know there was such a thing. Perhaps [the school] could publicize and explain our policies and standards of conduct to the entire faculty and student body so everyone can be informed."

"There are no woman department chairs—one female dean on campus. I want someone I can look up to, something to look forward to. I know there are not as many older female physicians as younger ones, but I wish I could meet them and be guided and mentored by them. What do I have to look forward to? Perhaps [the school] could facilitate interaction among students and faculty, both female and male."

These passages highlight again how deeply embedded patriarchy is within the structure of medical education as well as how much work will be needed to change the structure. Sexual harassment has received a large amount of press coverage in the media over the past few years, from the Anita Hill/Clarence Thomas confrontation to policies that specific colleges and universities have put into place to handle the problem. Sexual harassment policies, particularly in such male dominated fields such as medicine, should not be "news" to any member of any professional community, in the case of medical education, to students, faculty, or staff. That these policies are not common knowledge suggests that administration perceives that there is no need, that there is not a problem.

Women have entered the field of medicine in increasing numbers over the past few decades. Women now comprise over forty percent of medical students. However, their numbers at the general level have not translated into equivalent numbers at the top levels of administration. You can count the number of female medical school deans on one hand. At the medical school where I worked for eight years, there are no women sitting as chairs of departments, and there are only a few women division chiefs. There are now three women (out of fifteen) assistant or associate deans in the dean's office, two in Student Affairs. Women in positions of real authority are virtually non-existent. The processes of mentoring and sponsorship have largely taken care of male medical students, residents, and fellows. Women have not routinely been part of the networks that give rise to prominent positions for protégés.

The comments quoted above were confined to the first two years of medical school, yet these students have come head to head with the androcentrism and patriarchal structures that have defined and continue to define medical education today. Women students tell me that they are afraid to confront their professors for fear that the professors will remember them when it comes time to give grades or do clinical work in a setting where ratings are more subjective. Female clinicians that I have talked with about this agree that there is risk associated with such confrontation in this context.

Risks abound for faculty as well. When I discussed with colleagues the possibility of sending an open-ended invitation to former students in my gender-issues classes to bring me examples of sexual harassment, sexism, patriarchy and androcentrism that they had witnessed or experienced as medical students, several of them only half-jokingly expressed their hope that I really did not need a job because I probably would not have one for long if I sent such an invitation to students.

Because, ultimately, my dismissal would serve no one's interests—students or mine—I turned my attention to what I could do within the system we have to deal with. I realized that perhaps my goal of making a substantive contribution as a feminist in medical education could best be accomplished by continuing to give students a forum, albeit a small and quiet one, for discussing these issues openly. I have maintained an open door, open mind, and open ear for my past and present students over the years so that they talk freely when they come to my office or see me in the hallways. I have been able to listen, to hear, and I hope, to help by being available, putting them into contact with other faculty who may be in positions to help them, and by reminding them why they are in medical school. Perhaps another small contribution has been my unwillingness to reassure them with trite statements about how much better things are now than they were, say, fifteen years ago. An improvement in conditions does not justify conditions that are still unacceptable.

The exclusion and segregation experienced by women in medicine has not been reversed by the mass entry of women into the field of medicine over the past few decades. It is wishful thinking to believe that "co-education" means "equal" education and that increasing the numbers of women in medical schools will take care of the gender equity problem. What we need to accomplish beyond entry to medical school is equality of experiences (Tobias 1993) and outcomes for all students, regardless of gender, race, national origins, or sexual orientation. Numbers alone will not bring about change as long as power remains vested in one group. This is all too apparent as we look at the proportions of women in medicine today compared with the proportion of women in positions of authority, be it in medical schools (such as deans, department chairs, division chiefs), research institutes (such as the NIH), or societies (such as the Institute of Medicine or the American College of Surgeons).

At the medical school level, which is where I have spent the bulk of my professional time, I have tried to exercise my feminist commitment. I have come to see that change, if it is to come at all, will have to come from the top. I agree whole-heartedly with Dr. Frances Conley, the only female full professor of neurosurgery in the U.S., that "*nothing* will change in the world of medicine for women and minorities until there is a culture shift, and I have become absolutely convinced that the only true change of culture will come through the leaders we select. A racist and/or sexist tone at the top translates into validation of racism and sexism and perpetuates bigoted ideas for yet another generation" (1994, B3).

I would take this one step further by suggesting that even the most sensitive and supportive leadership will not be able to implement significant change without an open, honest, and thorough confrontation and examination of the patriarchal and androcentric structures of medicine and medical education. The value system(s) underlying the medical enterprise will not change with the formation of a university advisory committee on sexual harassment or the appointment of a women's liaison officer. It will not be enough to treat only the symptoms of the problem.

Men in medicine control the resources, the reward system, the structure, content and schedule of the experience as well as the professional networks. Medical education today remains androcentric and patriarchal. It reflects the attitudes, beliefs, and value systems embraced by the leadership. More feminists and more women must ascend to positions of leadership in medicine and medical education and make concerted efforts to exert their influence over the systems at hand. Women should not have to aspire to patriarchal standards, to conform to its values and standards, in order to achieve. We must look for patterns of achievement and not just focus on the occasional woman who has managed to succeed in the traditional way. We must be aware that we often may be our own worst enemies, for male dominance has taught us to question our own abilities and to play down our notable achievements. We must fight this form of internalized sexism (Mierson 1993).

Men and women must act on their feminist commitments individually and collectively. Women must have access to mentors, sponsors, and resources. This may become easier as more men in positions of authority find ways to help their daughters, sisters, and nieces who are entering the field of medicine, but we need strong feminists—male and female—to lead the way, to act on their commitments individually, and to organize collectively. Lorber (1984) reminds us that "personal solutions are vital for individuals to survive, but it takes concerted, politically sophisticated group action to restructure deeply embedded social arrangements" (114). Moreover, she writes, "gender discrimination is a pervasive and tightly woven structure that is for the most part impervious to individual actions. Yet the opposite side of the coin is that social patterns are constructed out of and maintained by individual actions" (Lorber 1984, x).

We cannot rely on those women who have risen to top positions by internalizing patriarchal leadership models to carry the banner of feminism in medical education. I do believe that change is possible, but as I noted at the beginning, change is slow. We must all, therefore, continue to work to break down patriarchal dominance in medicine and medical education, to make our own individual contributions to feminism in medical education, however seemingly small or invisible. Despite the odds against us, I believe that we do make a difference, and that it is these differences that give rise to the hope that the future will indeed be different.

Just how different, and how long we will have to wait to see these differences, remains to be seen. Those of us who try to make a difference face stiff resistance. In my own case, I have resisted patriarchy in medical education at one institution for eight years. I believe that I made a difference in the lives of individual students. But in the life of the institution? That is harder to say. On the one hand, I have had to strain for basics, such as a safe and healthy office environment and adequate staff to cover service functions that the school wants to offer but does not want to pay for. On the other hand, when I expressed my interest in attending the HERS Mid-America/Bryn Mawr College month-long residential professional development program for women in higher education administration, my participation was completely supported by the institution.

Perhaps most telling is what happened when my husband and I recently relocated to another part of the country. I resigned my position as Director of Continuing Medical Education as well as my faculty appointment. The resignation of my faculty appointment was not acknowledged at the department level. Did I feel invisible, unimportant, and ignored? Yes. Will the course continue? Probably, in the hands of a woman physician who has been marginalized within her own department.

My resignation as Director of CME and various contributions to the institution were warmly acknowledged by the Associate Dean to whom I reported. However, the position was then promptly moved from Academic Affairs to Graduate Medical Education. The individual who assumed my CME responsibilities was a man who worked in the dean's office developing quarterly extra-curricular seminars for medical residents. He had no administrative or CME experience, but his title now reads "Assistant Dean for Graduate and Continuing Medical Education." That's Assistant *Dean*, not Director, as I had been. With his appointment also came the news that the office would be moving to a far more desirable space: large, attractive, comfortable (and with a working ventilation system). Was this dehumanizing? Given the administration's knowledge of my aspirations with respect to higher education administration and my accomplishments? Yes, it felt that way. Did it hurt? You bet. Did it surprise me? Not at all.

Those who write the rules would have you believe that, as the 1950s television program proposed, "Father Knows Best." Those committed to feminism in medical education would have you believe otherwise. We have a long way to go.

CHAPTER 7

A Black Woman in Medicine

❑

Dale G. Blackstock

It was the first day of class at Harvard Medical School and I had this weird feeling of "what am I doing here?" When it came to education and career planning, there hadn't been any. All I ever remember is that after deciding (or being convinced that) I probably wouldn't make it as a nun or saint, the next challenging and exotic thing to do was to become a physician. I had always loved books, and the one thing I recall with fondness about my childhood was our trips to the library.

My family, which included my four brothers, a sister, and my mother, was no different from the next family in the inner-city where we lived. We were children who had been abandoned by our fathers and were being raised by our stressed-out but loving mothers. I can never remember our father living with us and I was never told why he left. My mother just never talked about it. We received support from ADC, otherwise known as welfare. It always seemed, according to my mother, that the welfare funds were inadequate. I recall her always dragging us down to the welfare office and ranting and raving about how difficult it was with so many mouths to feed. Once she actually left us sitting there, threatening the social worker that she would not take us back unless she received more money. She wasn't gone for more than fifteen minutes, but to a six-year-old it was an eternity. The social workers, called "investigators," were always snooping around our apartment looking for hidden luxuries such as a phone or other "unnecessary" electrical appliances.

During my early childhood, one of my most difficult obstacles was a severe stuttering problem. My mother's home remedy (we didn't know about speech pathologists in those days, but we couldn't have afforded one anyway) was to slap me hard in the mouth with her hand or a comb if she happened to be doing my hair when I attempted to talk. Frustrated, she would yell that I should shut up if I didn't know what I was going to say. So whenever I spoke in my mother's presence I had to be certain of what I was going to say, and the words had to come out without the usual stuttering. Eventually I overcame the stuttering but in its place I developed a deep fear of speaking in front of others, a fear that the words will not come out right or will not come out at all. To this day I can't ad lib, and must always be very well-prepared for presentations.

As the third oldest child, I tended to be quiet and shy, and in retrospect, the stuttering probably contributed to this state. The other reason was that by the time I reached the third grade, I had literally attended eight different schools. I was always the new kid on the block and never had the time to develop any unique friendships.

Except for several brief stints in the public school system, my formative educational years were spent in Catholic schools. After elementary school I attended Bishop McDonnell Memorial High school, an all girls Catholic school. There, a well-meaning nun told me that I should go into social work when I told her that I wanted to become a doctor. Perhaps she felt my 85 average was not sufficient for pursuing that profession.

Education was never stressed by my mother, who had barely completed high school. She had to worry about bigger things, such as rent and six mouths to feed. Yet her influence was deeply felt in our family in other ways. She always read the *Daily News* to my younger brother and sister, pointing out words and pictures to them. It must have helped because both were placed in gifted classes. But not just her children were bright. Years later she studied Licensed Practical Nursing, and passed her Boards on the first try without ever cracking a textbook. (She said she couldn't read the small print of her textbooks.) Still, she'd get nervous when I spent too much time studying, always reminding me to clean or do the dishes.

During high school, when there was a subliminal message bestowed on the students that women were meant to be loved and caring, I internalized these assumptions about the course of a woman's life. That is, she'd get married, have children, and live happily ever after. College was an option for me, only if marriage did not pan out. I didn't get married, so off I went to New York City Community College where I spent my first two years doing my liberal arts coursework, then to Brooklyn College where I majored in biology and completed my pre-med courses. At Brooklyn College I was lucky to have a chemistry professor, Dr. Clyde Dillard, who not only took me under his wing but encouraged and supported all African-American students. Many of us would not have gone on to medical school were it not for him. During my last two summers in college, I also got involved with the Harvard Health Career Summer Program (HCSP), a program for minorities interested in health fields that permitted us to take courses at Harvard.

After my experience with HCSP, I was confident enough to apply to medical school. Having done well at Brooklyn and on my MCAT, I got an early acceptance to Harvard Medical School. At Brooklyn I had been able to develop good study skills and had spent a great deal of time in the library; it had been hard to develop such skills at home in a room with six other people and the radio and the television on.

However, I was still guided by the wife-and-mother expectations that had been instilled in high school, and I *did* want to be a good wife and mother. And by high school standards, I was already four years behind in this goal. Reluctantly, I went off to medical school, but not before I had married my husband Earl and inherited an extended family.

Medical school was a blur. That time period reminds me of those movies where the months of the year flash rapidly across the screen, and years pass in what seems to be nanoseconds. We had decided that it would be best if Earl stayed in New York, but the commuting made it exceptionally difficult for me to get into the right frame of mind to study. This was a difficulty that continued throughout my four years at Harvard. The study skills I had whetted in college evaded me, and I took my share of exam make-ups.

In addition to these difficulties, medical school was a real culture shock for me. At that time, African-Americans represented ten percent of the class. Although the general attitude at the school was patronizing, the faculty gave a lot of attention and support to its students. (Being reticent I didn't take advantage of this; if I was having a problem with the material, I didn't know how to ask for help.) Contrary to what minority students have experienced at some other institutions, help was always available and no one felt threatened by the faculty. I was still rather withdrawn and afraid of stuttering in this new environment.

I was also somewhat intimidated by the backgrounds of many of my peers. Most of the students came from well-to-do families, including many of my African-American classmates. In my class alone, there was a student who was a relative of Jackie Onassis, several students whose parents had written textbooks that we would be using in class, several students who had parents on the faculty, a student whose father would win the Nobel Prize in Medicine in Immunology, and a student whose father was the co-inventor of the Swan-Ganz catheter. My claim to fame was my mother who received her LPN degree after raising six children, and I was very proud of her. She had attended school full-time, worked full-time, taken care of the family, and gotten off welfare.

There were never any overt racial incidents in medical school that I can recall. But a number of peculiar situations arose when I was not certain what was operating: sexism, classism, or racism. Professors still showed cheesecake slides and the women would jeer and hiss and a few of the men would join in; that was obviously sexism. But in other circumstances I was less sure. During one of my rotations with a white male student the professor held the door for the white student but let it slam in my face. Another time, when an off-color remark was made during the radiology conference, the professor apologized directly to my white female partner (her father was on the faculty and had written a definitive textbook); I was obviously invisible. Once during an informal breakfast my hand accidentally brushed against one of the pastries and out of the corner of my eye I saw the white resident throw it in the garbage. Another time after being up all night I was asked not to sleep in an empty patient room that held two beds (something that was done all the time) because the white resident was going to use the other bed. Or I think of the one white male patient who made no bones about not wanting a black student-doctor caring for him. I must say, however, that several of the white female surgical residents were very supportive and friendly. But by the time I finished medical school, I was exhausted.

My first day of internship at Harlem Hospital Center, I again had the weird feeling of wondering why I was there. Everything was surreal. I had just graduated from medical school and was now in charge of someone's life. I would be making life and death decisions, and it blew my mind.

Internship proceeded well enough, except that of the three of us who rotated on the ward, I always received the most admissions, usually four to five. These were never straightforward admissions but rather were complicated and required extensive management and hospital stays. And at Harlem Hospital, there was no limit to the hours an intern could work without sleep. In the midst of all this I became pregnant, and when I learned that I would be having twins, my only thought was to thank God they weren't triplets. I had hoped to make it to term without having to take time off, but with evidence of preeclampsia I went on leave in the seventh month. Of course, the interns rotating with me at the time never forgave me. I understood, and stayed out only four weeks after giving birth.

My first night on call after my return was the worst. I missed my baby daughters Oni and Uché (respectively "king" and "mind") very much. I wanted to give it all up and go home and just be a mother. But each night spent on call got better, and the horrible, terribly empty, aching feeling lessened. At home I was lucky to have help from a live-in woman, Ms. Criss, with whom I felt quite comfortable and confident. But she had this habit upon leaving each Friday of announcing that she wouldn't be coming back the following Monday because she couldn't handle both the babies and the household chores. I dreaded Mondays, and when I would hear Ms. Criss's key in the door, I knew things would be okay for one more week. To make matters even more hectic, it was during this time that my stepson Llew, who had special needs requiring attention, came to live with us.

To maintain my sanity, I started running quite intensively. While in Boston I had run ten to fifteen miles per week, but now I increased my weekly mileage to forty-two. I ran whenever I could. Late at night. Early in the morning. In the middle of the day if my schedule allowed it. I began entering races and became an even greater running freak. My goal at this point was to run a marathon, which I did. I got better and better, and was the first woman finisher in the 1978 Monmouth Marathon.

The Internal Medicine Boards loomed ahead, but my daughters and running were my priorities. Running was my outlet and to give it up would have been taking on a kamikaze mission. But when I didn't pass the first time, I knew I had to make a choice, running or passing the Boards.

Later during my residency, Ms. Criss had to go back to her country, Venezuela, for personal and business reasons, so at one-and-a-half years of age Oni and Uché were enrolled in "Little Sun People Nursery School." Each morning I dropped them off and they would bawl, which they did for the next two years whenever I dropped them off. After completing my residency, I took two years off from training and accepted a nine-to-five weekday medical consultation job. I was able to spend more evening and weekend time with the girls. I wanted the road to be easier for them than it had been for my sibs and me with all our various struggles. As I look at them now, I know they don't have the same anxieties I had, but I worry that maybe I made everything too intense for them. No TV during the week. On Saturdays violin lessons, music theory, and gymnastics. Then the library, Brooklyn Children's Museum, Prospect Park Rangers, and other places of interest.

After my two year hiatus I began my nephrology research fellowship at Brookdale Hospital Medical Center on an NIH grant. My great concern while in training was that Oni and Uché would receive the attention they deserved from their parents. They were now enrolled in a parochial school where discipline and rote memorization were emphasized. In retrospect I feel it was a bit too rigid for them, but the hours fit comfortably with our busy schedules. Even though they didn't cry when I dropped them off, I literally walked them into school for their first four years there.

After completing my fellowship, I spent the next four years as a medical specialist at Kingsboro Psychiatric Center and also ran the nephrology and hypertension clinic there. For the past six years I have been at SUNY Health Science Canter at Brooklyn in medicine and nephrology. Most of my time is spent in the clinic as attending and running the medical housestaff and fourth-year medical student Ambulatory Care elective. I search for adequate time to spend on clinical research projects and am presently involved in looking at kidney cyst in the black patient with end-stage renal disease. I am also president of Provident Clinical Society, the local chapter of the National Medical Association and an organization of 150–200 Brooklyn-based minority physicians.

Am I satisfied I went into medicine? Were there different pressures on me as a minority woman in medicine? Would I do things differently if I had it to do over again? Is medicine responsive to the needs of its physicians from varied cultural backgrounds?

Women in the medical profession face unique challenges when it comes to motherhood. We have to make excuses continuously because there is not enough support for us when family matters arise. Furthermore, I find that our opinions and contributions are not viewed as important as those of our male colleagues.

I enjoy medicine very much and would go into it again if I had to do it all over. In looking back, I believe that many of my negative experiences were the result of racism, not sexism. This is not to n i nimize the sluggishness of women's progress in medicine. But in this society , ice is such a major factor in our actions and policy-making that not to acknowledge it is unrealistic and naive.

Yet even black people have a difficult time seeing other black people in roles of authority. For example, I have had the experience of having a black patient tell me that his white doctor did so-and-so and that only his white doctor knew how to take care of him and handle his particular disease. A black male colleague of mine tells me that it is not uncommon for a black patient not to accept a diagnosis from him and to seek a second opinion. This request for a second opinion is tantamount to wanting an "audience" with a white doctor who will invariably give the patient the same information. The patient, however, is eminently more satisfied hearing the comments from a white doctor. Often this same friend has confronted such patients with their guile at which point they often apologize, vehemently.

Black people in this society learn to develop thick skin. Negative experiences must be turned into positive ones by seeing them as challenges and not as insurmountable obstacles. We learn to depend on inner strength to keep us on course. At the present time for my perseverance, stamina and fortitude, I look to my mother as my role model. I marvel at her as I do those countless black mothers who have achieved the unachievable.

I am honored to be a physician. That little six-year-old girl sitting in the welfare center would never have dreamed that one day she'd become a physician, let alone know what a physician was.

CHAPTER 8

The Feminization of Medicine

❑

Perri Klass

In the middle of my junior residency year, *The New York Times Magazine* invited me to write an article about women doctors. Their question, they said, was will women change medicine—or will medicine change women? The working title for this article, while I was writing it, was "The Feminization of Medicine."

I interviewed doctors about career patterns, about mentors and role models, about training issues, about families and children. One question I always asked, of course, was this: do you think women doctors do anything different? And one theme that emerged in the answers was that yes, many of the people I interviewed thought that overall there were some differences between the way women practice medicine and the way men do it. So I wrote that into the article with some trepidation—I was, after all, quoting women doctors on women doctors. I had done no scientific survey. But it was interesting, I thought, that within this group there seemed to be a sense of special pride.

The editor called and told me that the article would be on the cover of *The New York Times Magazine*, and the title would be "Why Women Are Better Doctors." After some negotiation, this was changed to read "Are Women Better Doctors?" Even so, it generated an enormous amount of angry mail, mostly from doctors, both male and female, most of whom had apparently read only the title. Several years later, when I spoke to a student group at Harvard Medical School, one young man told me that when he had read that article in college he had felt as if someone were saying to him, you won't be a very good doctor, you won't be the best.

I can't help thinking this is all pretty funny. What it reminds me of most, to tell you the truth, is when I was back in medical school, and went to a meeting with the director of admissions. I was there representing the women's student medical association, along with the people in charge of the black students' group, the Asian association, the Native American group, and the Gay

Students' Association. The director of admissions told us that he was very concerned that all our groups were sending out letters to students when they were accepted into the medical school, welcoming them, offering advice, and naming students to contact. He was concerned, he said, because no one was writing to the straight white men, and it didn't seem fair. There was a pause, and then someone said, in a mystified tone, "And still they keep coming!"

It seems to me that newspapers and magazines are still very much in the business of making women feel bad about having jobs. If you ask me, the whole "having it all" fuss is mostly just an excuse to warn you that if you have a job your personal life will suffer, your children will be deprived.

I found this in my journal from when I was working on this article:

> I picked up a magazine and found someone running on about the joys of staying home and someone else running on about how she gets no respect because she has no child. I mean, can you have it both ways? Either the moms are getting all the respect, since no childless woman is considered truly fulfilled, or else the career gals are getting all the respect, because only money and career count in this soulless society, or else everyone just likes to whine. Everyone just likes to whine. I like the amazed surprise of women who discover that having a baby while working full-time means either leaving the baby to go to work or else not working, and I like the amazed surprise of women who discover that staying home full-time leaves them without an exciting job to go to. But what more worthwhile job could I be doing? they ask. Well, they could be helping those in need, or writing nonwhiney columns, or repairing broken machinery. Or else staying home, if that is more fun. Who cares? I can see I'm not going to get very far in the dilemma-of-the-professional-woman market.

Every article about a successful woman dwells on the tragedies and failures of her private life, while articles about successful men jump blithely over marriages that came to nothing, children left by the wayside. Certainly, no one ever writes about men in a way that suggests that because they have remained uncoupled everything else they have achieved is worthless. No one suggests that because they did not spend enough time with their babies, their accomplishments are ashes in their mouths. I was glad to contribute an article that weighed in on the other side. And someday when men are a minority in medicine, no doubt there will be an enterprising journalist who will examine the phenomenon of the male doctor, and wonder whether men bring any special strengths to the profession.

Are Women Better Doctors?

There was a conundrum which used to turn up now and then, when I was in high school, designed to test your level of consciousness: a father and son go fishing, and on the way home, they're in a car accident. The father is killed instantly, the boy is rushed to the hospital, where the surgeon takes one look at him and screams, "Oh, my God, it's my son!" What is the relationship between the surgeon and the child?

Well, obviously, the surgeon is the child's mother. Surely no one had to think twice about that? Well, fifteen years ago, lots of people would ponder that puzzle, making up complex stepfather/grandfather linkages, trying to explain how a child could have no father, but still have a parent who was a doctor.

In 1969, 9.2 percent of the first-year medical students in America were women; in 1987 it was 36.5 percent. In 1970, women accounted for 7.6 percent of all the physicians in America and 10.7 percent of the residents. In 1985, 14.6 percent of all physicians and 26.2 percent of all residents were female. Perhaps the most important and most interesting questions that confronts female M.D.'s as they become more and more a fact of life in the medical profession is this: are women actually changing medicine, are they somehow different as doctors—or does the long and rigorous medical training produce doctors who are simply doctors, male or female?

I did not go to medical school during the pioneering age. When I started, in 1982, 53 of the 165 students in their first year at Harvard Medical School were women. Moreover, I chose to go into pediatrics, a field that has the highest percentage of female residents of any medical specialty—fifty percent nationwide. I have never had the experience of being the only woman in the lecture hall, the only female resident in the hospital. Occasionally, I have been the only woman on a particular medical team, but often I have been on all-female teams. During my own medical training, so far at least, I have not had reason to feel like a scholarship student from an alien tribe. When I set out to write about women in medicine, I wanted to bypass the tone of patronizing surprise that so often attends women doing untraditional jobs ("She uses a scalpel! She has curly blond hair and a white coat all covered with blood!"). I also wanted to leave behind some of the classic topics that apply various kinds of prurience to the situation of the female doctor. So what's it like when you have to do a physical exam on a man? So how do women doctors get along with nurses? And so on. With women going into medicine in large numbers, it's time to look more specifically at what kinds of doctors we are choosing to be, both in terms of specialty and in terms of style.

According to data compiled by the Association of American Medical Colleges, men and women applying to medical school have similar acceptance rates—of all applicants to medical school for the year starting in September 1986, 60.5 percent of the men were accepted into at least one school, and 59.6 percent of the women. After medical school, you choose your field of medicine. Here, men and women differ, according to statistics compiled for 1986. Fifty percent of all pediatric residents were women, but only 11.8 percent of all surgical residents were female, and in vascular surgery it was only 1.4 percent (that added up to one woman in the country). Women are still heavily concentrated in psychiatry (40 percent of the psychiatric residents in the U.S. in 1986 were female), and also make up large proportions of the residents in dermatology (43.9 percent), preventive medicine (36.2 percent), pathology (37.5 percent), and obstetrics and gynecology (45.1 percent). The "frontier" for women in medicine, then is really not in medical school but in some of the medical specialties, in which they are almost as rare as they ever were. The traditionally acceptable areas for women doctors (pediatrics, psychiatry) are still attracting large numbers of women. Speaking as a pediatrician, I know that one reason I like my field is because of all the women, both at my own level and up ahead of me, already established. But how does my experience then compare to someone else's training in surgery?

It seems to be pretty well agreed that back when there were fewer women in medicine, medical school and residency were often fraught with unpleasantness and loneliness; many women have written about the sexual innuendoes, the what's-a-nice-girl-like-you comments, the exclusion, the sense of being singled out and put on the spot—all the petty persecutions that added up to anger and alienation. On the other hand, while the more recent medical school graduates I interviewed could remember incidents, individual rotten professors, bad moments, none felt she had been the victim of any real discrimination in medical school. However, in those specialties where a woman is still a rarity, all those old problems may still confront the resident or the young doctor trying to get started in practice. Furthermore, there are very few women in the upper echelons of academic medicine: in 1987, two medical schools had female deans (out of 127); seventy-eight academic departments (out of approximately two thousand) had female chairs.

In examining the position of women in medicine, I talked to many women doctors. Some are colleagues of mine, teachers of mine, friends of friends in the vast and complex Boston teaching hospital system. But Boston is hardly a typical place to learn or practice medicine. Affectionately and not so affectionately referred to as "Mecca," Boston is the most heavily academic city for medicine in the U.S., probably in the world. (A cartoon used to hang on the wall of the residents' room in the intensive care unit of the hospital where I work: a scientist is scrawling complex equations on a blackboard, respectfully watched by a group of fellow scientists. In balloons we see the thoughts of his audience; each one is thinking "What is he doing?" And the scribbler himself is thinking, "What the hell am I doing?" In big letters on the top of this cartoon, someone had printed, MECCA.) The female experience in medicine in Boston can never be considered typical. Some people will swear that women have it easy in Boston because medicine here is dynamic, young, on the cutting edge; and others will insist that nowhere is the old boy network stronger than in the Boston hospitals.

I told a friend—a fellow resident—that I was writing about women doctors. "What are you going to say?" she wanted to know. "Are you going to say they're better? Are you going to come right out and say it?" Now, if I read an article saying that men make better doctors than women for certain reasons, I would probably be offended, even hurt. The best I might hope for would be to laugh it off as so much antediluvian their-egos-are-threatened prejudice. Now, I have known superb, brilliant, sensitive male doctors, residents my own age, teachers and attending physicians. Lots of them. The doctor who delivered my son and the pediatrician who takes care of him are men—and yet, I feel I am protesting too much, that these statements have a some-of-my-best-friends air about them. Okay, then, some of my best friends are male doctors.

When I interviewed women doctors, I came always to the point where I asked, are women doctors different? And with only a couple of exceptions, I got versions of the same response from the doctors I interviewed, young or old, avowedly feminist or not. First you get that disclaimer, the one I just offered; I've known some wonderful male doctors, I've known some awful female doctors, generalizations are impossible. And then, hesitantly, even apologetically, or else frankly and with a smile, comes the generalization. Yes, women are different as doctors: they're better.

Kansas City announces proudly in the courtesy magazine found in fancy hotel rooms: "When Proctor & Gamble wants to know if people like its toothpaste, it turns to Kansas City. Market researchers call Kansas City a 'typically American' market. The label fits: Kansas Citians thrive on family, hard work, and tradition." In Kansas City, I interviewed a wide range of female doctors—residents, women just out of residency starting up private practices, academic physicians, specialists, older women, and recent graduates. I was surprised by how tight the network of women physicians was. I was immediately referred from doctor to doctor; in specialties where there were fewer women, their names were mentioned again and again by their colleagues. I was able to interview female physicians who stood on both sides of two classic relationships: a mentor and her student protégée, a doctor and her patient—who was also a doctor.

Linda Dorzab started medical school at the University of Missouri, Kansas City, when she was thirty-three years old. She had spent eleven years as a teacher, working with emotionally disturbed children. In June 1987, she finished her internal medicine residency, and is now beginning a private practice as an internist, affiliated with Menorah Medical Center. For the first month or so there were few patients, maybe only one a day, but by February it was up as high as nine a day, mostly new patients coming for their first appointments with her. Dr. Dorzab is proud to make a visitor welcome in her newly arranged office; an ebullient, friendly, informal woman, completely delighted to be starting up a new solo private practice. Ever since she started medical school, she says, she has dreamed of an office where she could make her patients comfortable, where there would be an atmosphere that would make her look forward to coming to work in the morning. Her office is a welcoming, plant-filled place, with gleaming mahogany furniture, including both a large desk and a small table designed for less threatening, more comfortable doctor-patient conversations. I, in the middle of my residency, find myself asking how she figured out the details of starting a practice—what supplies to order, how to find patients. Dr. Dorzab laughs, remembering how she sat down and made a list—"Cotton pads, tongue depressors—I ordered too many syringes and needles. And my proudest possession is my sigmoidoscope" (a device inserted up through the patient's rectum to give the doctor a good look at the lining of the colon). Given her background in working with disturbed children, Dr. Dorzab had originally considered going into psychiatry, "but they gave me a stethoscope and it was all so interesting. You can't get more interesting than medicine." She was older than most of the other students, and had a comparatively weak science background, but the art of medicine, she thinks, came more easily to her than to some of the younger students. Still, she had trouble performing on rounds, the high-pressure on-the-spot situations which can often be the traditional hazing occasions for medical students. "I still have the same personality as when I was a teacher, I tend to show my vulnerability—which is okay with my patients. But with colleagues the smile dims, I can turn on a more businesslike manner."

I asked her about role models, mentors, teachers from medical school who meant a lot to her. She names two women, saying of both of them that "they maintained femininity and class, and always looked confident." One of those women was Dr. Marjorie Sirridge, who is a dean at Dr. Dorzab's alma mater, UMKC. Marjorie Sirridge graduated from medical school in 1944. There were very few women in her class, but she never felt what she considers overt discrimination. To be sure, her academic advisers told her she'd never get to medical school—but that only made her more determined to go. "I was first in my class from grade one through high school—that gives confidence." Sure enough, she graduated from medical school first in that class too. But during residency she got pregnant and was informed that "pregnant residents were not acceptable." She dropped out of medicine for several years, then found her way back in by working for no pay and no training credit, went into private practice as a hematologist, pursued research on her own, and eventually found her way to academic medicine. Dr. Sirridge's office is decorated with pictures of her children and a poster of Marie Curie. Her white hair is bound up in a knot. She is extremely cordial, but she speaks with the authority of someone who is accustomed to giving out her opinions publicly. It is clear that she feels protective about the medical students she watches over, and that she is proud of Dr. Dorzab, who is striking out on her own, off into solo practice.

Dr. Sirridge worries that female medical students do not seem to take leadership roles as readily as their male colleagues. On the other hand, she thinks women do much better when it comes to human relationships. "For the women, relationships with patients are very important, a very positive thing. Many men also have this quality, but men in positions of power in medical education and government by and large do not."

The craving for female role models, female mentors, is very strong in medicine. You learn science in medical school—biochemistry, physiology, pathology; you learn these subjects in traditional classroom settings. Then you serve a kind of apprenticeship in the hospital for the second two years of medical school, consolidating the science you learned in the lecture hall, learning hospital logic and medical routine, and also learning how to be a doctor. How will you explain to a patient that he has to undergo a painful diagnostic procedure, how will you tell parents their child is dying, how will you help someone overcome bad habits that are crippling his health, how will you take command when someone is critically ill? Some medical schools are trying, more and more, to teach these skills, or at least to get students thinking and talking about them, instead of just piecing their styles together as they go along. But basically, since there is no single consensus on the best manner of doctoring, you pick up your style by trying to emulate the doctors you admire. And if you're female, it can be very instructive (and very inspiring) to watch women doctors, to learn your style from them. Many of the techniques used traditionally by male doctors tend not to work for women; and many female doctors have found themselves evolving new ways of interacting with patients, with nurses, with fellow doctors. So it isn't just vague inspiration that we're talking about here, it's who you're thinking of as you get ready to walk into that room and tell those parents about their baby dying. Who do you know who could do that as well as it could be done, offer comfort to the parents, inspire trust that their baby's last moments will be made as comfortable and easy as possible—how do you acknowledge their grief, the failure of medicine to help, even take part in their grief, and yet retain the authority you need as the doctor? And how much authority *do* you need as the doctor, anyway? Medicine is full of these situations, and you model yourself on the people who seem to handle them best.

Nevada Mitchell, M.D., practices internal medicine. Her subspecialty is geriatrics. She was born in Kansas City, went to college at Vassar, then came back to KC, got married, started teaching—she had thought about medical school, but didn't feel she had what it would take to go. But reading in the Vassar alumnae magazine about classmates who had gone to medical school, she decided she wanted to try for it, and five years later she was in medical school. Dr. Mitchell has no doubt at all about the difference between male and female doctors. "There's a world of difference. The women I come into contact with are less aggressive, more likely to have one-on-one-type relationships with patients than men, less likely to go for high volume of patients—but also less likely to be out here in private practice." Dr. Mitchell returned several times to the issue of being "out here," explaining that many women take jobs with HMOs, which offer regular salaries and limited working hours. "You need a certain aggressiveness to choose private practice," she said, with some satisfaction.

Dr. Mitchell feels that older patients are often more receptive to women doctors, since they are looking for more than medical therapy. Her original decision to go into geriatrics was related to watching her younger colleagues in medical school trying to deal with the many elderly patients, and feeling those patients were often neglected or taken for granted. Her medical practice now includes many older patients, but she also does general internal medicine. With a smile, she ticked off the various groups on her fingers: older people are fine, younger and middle-aged women usually have no problem with a female doctor, younger men are initially hesitant, feel self-conscious about the complete physical examination.

Dr. Mitchell cannot think of a female doctor she wanted to be like. "I didn't have that many examples. I developed my own style and image." She did, however, tell me that I ought to talk to the doctor who had operated on her when she needed some gynecological surgery. She felt that when she had discussed the medical issues with a male doctor, he had placed less of a priority on maintaining the option of future pregnancy. Dr. Mitchell, who is thirty-nine and has a sixteen-year-old daughter, wanted to keep her options open, and felt that a female doctor, Marilyn Richardson, had been more willing to take this seriously.

Ironically, Dr. Richardson herself thinks that's nonsense. An obstetrician-gynecologist specializing in reproductive endocrinology, she was a pianist for years before she went to medical school. She is highly professional, authoritative, and decided in her opinions. Patients who come looking for a female gynecologist, she says, are "erroneous—it's a patient's misconception that has evolved with consumer awareness, an erroneous belief that women doctors are more compassionate, more understanding. Well, I don't have menstrual cramps, I didn't have severe pain in labor. Women who come asking for a female doctor are looking for a buddy, and they're not going to find that in me."

I repeat to her what Dr. Mitchell said, and she laughs and says with affection, "Nevada Mitchell played the violin in my first piano recital." And then continues to deny that being female has anything to do with her mode of doctoring. "It was a male mentor who taught me sensitivity toward the preservation of fertility." Her style, she says, is a composite of this mentor and of her father, also in Ob-Gyn, and of techniques of doctoring she has developed for herself.

I mention to Dr. Richardson that one of the places I always felt a very sharp difference between male and female doctors was in the operating room. I ask whether she believes this is also erroneous. No, she agrees, the way that women run an OR is different. "Women manage more efficiently if they can strike a balance of authoritativeness and humaneness. Men are often arbitrary, demanding, and disrespectful, and the level of efficiency suffers. Women don't usually command quite as fiercely, will *ask* for an instrument . . . you get camaraderie with the other staff members."

Dr. Susan Love agrees. One of the first two female surgical residents at a major Boston teaching hospital, Dr. Love finished her training in 1980. She went into private practice in general surgery, though she initially had trouble getting a position on the staff of the hospital where she had just been chief surgical resident. In her practice, she found she was seeing many patients with breast disease, who preferred to go to a woman doctor, and she eventually decided to specialize in this field. She now has a partner, another woman surgeon, and they have as many patients as they can handle. Dr. Love feels strongly that she had to suppress many of her basic values in order to get through her surgical residency: "Most women have problems—unless they can block out their previous socialization. Surgeons don't really like having women, don't make it comfortable for them. Things that women like, talking to patients, aren't important, it's how many operations you've done, how many hours you've been up, how many notches on your belt. If you get through your five or six years of training, you can regain your values, but it's a real if. Most men never get them back."

Dr. Love runs an operating room, she says, by "treating the nurses like intelligent people, talking to them, teaching them. I'm not the big ruler." Are men always so different? "Surgery is a lot of ritual and a little science. The boys need high mass, incense, and altar boys, they need more boosting up. The women are much lower church." A concrete example of something she does differently, something no one taught her: before the patient is put to sleep, she makes it a practice to hold the patient's hand. "I'm usually the only person in the room they really know, and it's the scariest time. The boys scrub, come in when the patient's asleep. I got razzed for it, but they're used to it now."

Unlike Dr. Richardson, Dr. Love does think that women doctors behave differently with their patients. "I spend more time in empathy, talking, explaining, teaching, and it's a much more equal power relationship." And then there's not taking people for granted—she tells the story of a recent patient, an eighty-four-year-old woman with breast cancer who was asked by a male surgeon, "Are you vain?" Embarrassed, the woman said she wasn't. The surgeon advised her, in that case, to have a mastectomy, rather than a more limited procedure—"But then her niece pointed out, but you bought a new bra to come to the doctor, but you combed your hair over your hearing aid." The doctor had simply assumed that an elderly woman would have no particular desire to keep her breast, no vanity left to speak of. Dr. Love's anecdotes are often sharp—she describes a male surgeon who explained that a particular implant used in breast reconstruction felt just like a normal breast; he meant, of course, that to some-one touching the breast, the texture was close to natural, not that the woman actually had normal feeling in the implant.

I heard over and over that women are better at talking to people, better at listening. Dr. Carol Lindsley, a rheumatologist at the University of Kansas, says the female medical students are "more sensitive to patient and family needs, more patient, pay more attention to detail." Dr. Marilyn Rymer, a Kansas City neurologist, says that many of her female patients come looking for a woman doctor, some because they feel they can talk to a woman more easily, others because "they find that women listen better, are more empathic, care about explaining things, dealing with the family." Dr. Dorzab agrees: "My patients say women listen better, are better at acknowledging when something is both-ering the patient." On the other hand, Dr. Debbie Stanford, a resident in inter-nal medicine at the University of Alabama in Birmingham, feels that there is no difference at all between the male and female interns she supervises: "Capabil-ities, compassion, endurance—no difference." And Dr. Michelle Harrison, who wrote *A Woman in Residence* in 1982 about her experiences doing an Ob-Gyn residency, comments, "I think women sometimes *feel* different because they are not totally accepted; as outsiders, we experience ourselves as different, but are we all that different in how we see patients? I don't see any major rev-olution."

Then there is the question of how women get along with their co-work-ers—with other doctors and with nurses. The assumption has traditionally been that nurses resent female doctors, respond to them with a why-should-I-take-orders-from-*her* attitude, and then there are prurient little remarks about how women doctors resent nurses because of all the romantic attention the nurses supposedly receive from the male doctors.

Women doctors, of course, are often mistaken for nurses; many patients assume that a woman with a stethoscope is by definition a nurse. Some doctors mind this, others take it in stride. "You have to have a sense of humor," said Dr. Lois J. McKinley, an internist in Kansas City. "I took care of one patient for weeks, and when he was getting ready to leave, he was still saying, 'Oh, nurse, would you prop up my pillows.' Nursing people are good people; being mistaken for a nurse is not the worst thing that could happen." Dr. Mitchell agrees: "If I walk into a room and someone asks me for a bedpan, I just go ahead and put 'em on it!" She is laughing. "But when they call my office and assume I'm the nurse and ask, Dr. Mitchell, when will he be in, I tell them, '*He* will never be in!'"

It is generally agreed, among women doctors, that we have to be more polite and more careful with nurses than our male colleagues; a fairer way of putting this would probably be to say that nurses have had to take a lot of rudeness and bad behavior from doctors over the years, and that while they make some of the traditional female allowances for traditional male patterns, they are unwilling to accept these same behaviors from women. Or, to quote Dr. Richardson again, "When you make a big mess in the operating room, there's something different in your mind when you walk out and leave it for another woman to clean-up." I have found in my own training that nurses generally expect me to clean-up after myself (i.e., to gather up all the little alcohol pads and pieces of gauze left on the bed after I draw blood from a baby), to do a fair amount of my own secretarial work, and not to take too high-and-mighty a tone. What would be taken as normal behavior in a male (especially a male surgeon; they have the most traditional doctor-nurse power structure) is considered aggressive and obnoxious in a female. Dr. Lore Nelson, who will be chief resident in pediatrics at the University of Kansas next year, complained, half-seriously, "A male surgeon can walk in to do some procedure and everything will be all ready, but if I go to draw blood, nothing's set up for me and I have to go ask a nurse, 'Can you please help me . . .'" Dr. Sirridge agrees: "The women aren't successful at doing the things men do without criticism—it's easier if they ask politely."

This does not seem to be a bad thing—the traditional doctor-nurse relationship, like the traditional male-female relationship that is parodied (the man as authority figure, making decisions, issuing edicts, bearing ultimate responsibility on his broad shoulders; the woman as caretaker, tending to immediate needs and cleaning up messes, but without any real power) left a lot to be desired. Surely a good doctor is part caretaker; surely a good nurse's observations should be part of any decisions being made. I suspect that the more polite, more politic behavior that is demanded of female doctors may be closer to good manners and good medicine than the supposed norm—the license that we sometimes envy our male colleagues.

"Cleaning-up messes," a number of doctors told me, is something women do well. "Women are better at dealing with the nitty-gritty," says Dr. Sirridge, because they have been taught to clean-up, "to do the dishes at home. They tolerate tedious nitty-gritty-type things better." Medicine is full of messes, both palpable (the patient is dirty, the patient is vomiting, the patient is having bloody stools) and impalpable (the patient is ready to be discharged but has no home to go to, the child is medically healthy but will not eat). Some doctors do hold themselves aloof from these messes, seeing their role as something exclusively medical and dignified ("I didn't go to medical school to learn to clean up vomit"). And women do tend to be better at dealing with messes; it is more often what they have been raised to do, less likely to compromise their dignity, less likely to jar their image of themselves.

Medical training and medical practice are stressful for everyone, male and female. Women often face additional pressures; the issue of combining family and career comes up constantly when you try to write about women in medicine. Why are there discrepancies in status? For example, one study looked at medical school faculty (those with M.D.'s only, excluding those with Ph.D's or other degrees) given their first appointments in 1976. By 1987, 17 percent of the men were tenured, but only 12 percent of the women. Twelve percent of the men had attained the rank of full professor, but only 3 percent of the women. And 15 percent of the men were not on a tenure track at all, as compared with 22 percent of the women. So either women are meeting prejudice and resistance as they try to make their way in the world of academic medicine and research, or else, as is often suggested, they are diluting their ambition, going more slowly on their climb, usually in order to give time to family. Dr. Harrison, now a family physician and psychiatrist, feels that there are different standards for men and women. "Personality factors enter into the promotion of women, while arrogant and obnoxious men are promoted without that being an issue." But she also thinks that women "have tremendous problems around leadership, issues of power. We aren't raised with the skills to even make it up to the glass ceiling." And finally, she adds, "there's the problem of how to combine a family with a medical career, which tends to relegate women to salaried positions with less possibility for advancement."

I had my baby in the second year of medical school; it was not an extremely common thing to do, but neither was it unheard of. Certainly, I didn't feel any pressure to drop out, to take time off, to get my belly out of sight. I didn't feel it would be held against me, or against women in medicine, for me to have a baby along the way, and for that I suppose my medical school and the changing times deserve a lot of credit. Dr. Sirridge got pregnant during her internal medicine residency in the nineteen forties and had to drop out—"Pregnant residents were not acceptable." In my residency program there are several pregnant residents; the program is not particularly designed to accommodate them, but it seems to have been stretching. On the other hand, that's pediatrics again, a field with lots of women, a field where even the biggest guns have to be committed to the idea that babies are important.

Residents work nights and come home rarely and in poor condition. Many programs don't have much coverage available in case of sickness; there's a macho ideology that gives points for working when you're sick. So taking days off to stay home with a sick child is really against the rules, and ends up loading more work on your already overloaded fellow residents, which in turn creates animosity toward people with children. Nevada Mitchell's daughter was three years old when her mother started medical school, seven when she started residency. A single mother, she chose her residency program because she could live in the same building as her brother and sister-in-law, requested Friday night call because she didn't have to get up and bring her daughter to school the next day. When her daughter got sick and she decided to stay home, the attending physician commented, "Interns don't stay home unless they're hospitalized or dead." Dr. Mitchell stayed home for that one day only, then sent her daughter, who had mononucleosis, off to stay with relatives. "One Halloween we spent in the CT scanner," Dr. Mitchell recalls. "I brought her candy and her trick-or-treat bag."

Most annoying of all, perhaps, for parents, is that being a doctor makes you in a certain sense unreliable. Emergencies come up, unexpected calls come in, and you're home hours later than you promised; you can't keep the promise you made about a family outing. "She knows she can't depend on me to be where I say I'm going to be at any particular time or to be home when I say I'm going to be. She has to catch me when I'm there." When Dr. Mitchell opened her practice, her daughter would come by the office after school and they would go home together. Her daughter, who is now sixteen, wants to be a veterinarian.

These difficulties are not, of course, unique to the women. Males also have to cope with the hours, with not being there when their children need them, with promises made and broken. They are somewhat more likely to have spouses who delay their own careers. Still, I have heard complaints about male colleagues of mine who are too eager to leave the hospital and get home to their families; some men may even be much less self-conscious about this precisely because they bear no if-I-make-a-fuss-about-my-kid-they'll-think-women-shouldn't-be-doctors burden. No one, after all, is likely to say that fatherhood and medicine don't mix. The fact is, though, that certain intensities of career are essentially incompatible with any kind of parenthood. You don't have very much to do with your child if your ideal is to spend every waking moment in the hospital, whether you are the father or the mother. The influx of women into medicine, we can hope, will help us design medical careers for both men and women that will enable doctors to follow some of their own recommendations (reduce stress, eat a healthy diet, keep regular ours, spend time with your family—we pediatricians, for example, are always telling parents how important it is that they pay lots of attention to their children). Dr. Nelson is married to another doctor, who is doing his residency in internal medicine. She had a baby in her second year of residency, and felt that her fellow residents were very helpful and supportive. She and her husband had been in the habit of taking call on the same nights, so they would be home on the same nights; since the baby, they take call on alternate nights. Her husband, she thinks, has had much more trouble with his colleagues than she did: "The times he had to stay home when the baby was sick the men he worked with said, your wife should stay home."

After residency, many doctors continue to work long hours, to cover night call. One way to keep your hours regular is to work for an HMO. Another solution for doctors who want protected time for their families is a part-time practice. Anne Regier, M.D., and Perry Ginder, M.D., are rheumatologists in practice together in Kansas City. Each works three days a week and they split night coverage. Dr. Regier is married to an orthopedic surgeon. "We do a lot of juggling," she says. "I'll bring the kids to the hospital and drop them off with you so you can do your consult—or who will round first on the weekend."

Women are a presence in American medicine today in such numbers that in many fields they are no longer curiosities. Not being a curiosity gives you a certain amount of freedom; you don't have to be better than the men, you don't have to pretend that you actually are a man in disguise. But questions remain. Will women move ahead into positions of leadership? Are there subtle prejudices that will allow us the M.D. degrees, but then shunt us into the less prestigious career paths within medicine? Will the remaining all-male fields ever integrate? Janet Bickel, senior staff associate and director for women's studies at the AAMC, wonders whether we will in fact end up with a medical establishment in which certain jobs (less well paid, less well regarded) will be filled largely by women. And to what extent does this depend on the choices made by the women themselves? It is very difficult to make predictions; the makeup of the medical profession has changed so rapidly from this point of view that there is really no way to say what will happen next.

Many women doctors believe that women do medicine differently, that there are advantages to the way they approach their patients. Almost no doctor I talked to believes that women have simply been transformed by their medical education into cookie-cutter doctors with all the mannerisms and techniques of the male prototype. If this is in fact true, and not just a convenient prejudice on our part (and one I still blush to acknowledge in print), then the effect of women on the medical profession may be larger and more far-reaching than we have yet imagined.

Recently I told my four-year-old son that he was due for a check-up with his pediatrician. He looked distinctly nervous (rumors about shots had obviously been making their way around the day-care center), and asked me anxiously, "Is she a nice doctor?" I thought about the doctors my son knows—me, my close friends, mostly female. I picked my words carefully; it was clearly one of those critical moments when all of a mother's wisdom and tact is required. "Benjamin," I said, "I have to tell you something. Boys can be doctors too, if they want to. If they go to school and learn how, boys can be very good doctors, really."

CHAPTER 9

If the Suit Fits . . .

❑

Kate H. Brown

A vivid image of a little girl dressed in a man's suit came to me one day when I was trying to finish the syllabus for a course I was teaching for medical students at the University of California at Berkeley. I was stuck. Whenever I forced concentration on the task, a heavy feeling of boredom descended like a sedative and my mind would wander out of focus. Only a week left before the class began, I kept dragging away from daydreams to concentrate on getting something—anything—on the page. But invariably I would slip again into the dulled void of procrastination, past controlled thought, past time.

The image of the little girl appeared during the last of these go arounds. She stood there, vulnerable and small in a disheveled, oversized suit with the cuffs and sleeves rolled-up over her ankles and wrists. She smiled quizzically and declared that she would do her best if this is what I really wanted from her. Her sweet, pathetic stance made me laugh out loud, but even while laughing I realized the seriousness of her message. I had been trying to write a syllabus for someone else's class, not mine. She was wearing the suit of George Foster, the esteemed elder "father" of my field, medical anthropology, and I had been trying to do the class as I imagined he would do it. Her image faded as I assured her gently that I would not ask her to wear his suit. I threw out the old plans, and a new course took shape effortlessly in no time.

I later told the students this story, explaining why the seminar content and process would be a bit different from their usual fare. We decided together what topics to cover in the course according to their interests and curiosities within the discipline. The students also shared responsibility for developing a variety of assignments and class interactions that encouraged collaborative, reflective, and experiential learning. They threw themselves into the class with enthusiasm, and we all learned a great deal from one another that semester. I love to teach like that.

Of course, veering from the norm was the norm for the Berkeley experience of medical education where classes of twelve students take three years to combine a Master's degree with their academic medical training. Students enrolled in this UCB/UCSF Joint Medical Program receive their M.D. after completing two final years of clinical training at the University of California at San Francisco. My feminist teaching experiments were not so radical in this context.

Teaching in a Traditional Medical School

Harder "suit tests" have come since joining the faculty in a traditional medical school in the midwest. At Creighton University I teach the required second semester of ethics and health policy in the Fall of the students' second year. Even with the considerable pedagogical comprises I have made to accommodate medical school requirements, traditions, and class size (120), mine is a different sort of class.

Influenced by the emerging traditions of feminist pedagogy (Stone 1994) and feminist ethics (Sherwin 1992), my teaching strategies are intended to engage students with the complexities of their own values and motivations in the context of real life. In this course, my specific concern is with an ethic of service. As a Jesuit University, the concept of service is highlighted in the language of the mission statement, but (thankfully) it is not defined. I have designed the course to encourage students to come to their own definitions of service through reflection, dialogue, and experiential explorations and practice.

There are good theoretical reasons for teaching this way, but it is a logistics whirlwind. The bulk of their grade involves pass/fail writing assignments. Some students choose to write journal entries about their interviews and service in community shelters and clinics; others write letters to the editor about a current policy debate affecting their notion of an ethic of service; others write commentaries about the depiction of service in literature. Class sessions include lectures, panel discussions, and facilitated small group discussions. Before each group discussion, students write a page on their impressions, feelings, and opinions about the assigned story or policy analysis.

I purposefully oppose the reductionist traditions of medical education and medical ethics in this class. Instead of abstract clarity and simplicity, I teach ethics as something forged from the dynamic swirl of political and economic influences which need to be appreciated and weighed in light of one's moral and medical judgments, upbringing, personal commitments, and emotional state. This approach is not easy for many of the students whose competence in other classes depends on their systematic attention to precise pieces of neatly interlocking systems—not critical, self-reflexive, open-ended analysis. Consequently, I am careful to balance the open-ended and exploratory nature of their assignments, discussions, and exams with structured deadlines and detailed explanations of my expectations. This helps carry students through their initial confusion to meaningful personal insight. But every semester I re-recognize that the course content and my style of teaching will always be peripheral in a curriculum that reflects a very different paradigm of knowledge and teaching. The realization is not always a happy moment. My frustrations and sense of alienation are illustrated in this entry from my journal last year as I examined a comment from one of my students.

> "Ethics is just a can of worms." A can of worms?
>
> Her words bring images of fetid and tangled masses of worms left to strangle themselves on each other, the fisherman long gone from the scene. She is right. Our discussions, if they are done well, do release strong feelings, disagreements, often a sense of powerlessness, confusion, contingencies, everyday pitfalls for integrity, and unending ambiguities brought to light from the safety of their confines, no longer preserved and intact.
>
> Her unspoken accusation rings loud. What she really meant to say is, "How do you expect us to pass our other courses with minds so unsettled by dangerous places and impossible choices?" She is right again. How could I have forgotten in medical education there is only one correct answer on a multiple choice exam?

The temptation to wear another's suit persists at the start of each new semester. Maybe, I think, this time I could get away with the straightforward "received knower" model (Belenky et al. 1986) of learning that characterizes their other courses. This is the usual sort of teaching in our school: the teacher talks and assigns portions of the text to memorize, students receive knowledge from these sources, and are evaluated on a computerized exam of the material. Lab work augments their learning experience in some classes. I am tempted to believe it could work if I would teach ethics with the detached certainty of teachers schooled in western traditions of analytical philosophy. I'm not proud of this desire to slip into conformity, but to do so would save me a load of work and emotional intensity and probably not change the students' numerical ratings of the class. Of course I would prefer to project a picture of a dedicated feminist in the trenches of male dominance and hierarchy who unstintingly lights the torches of reflexive self-knowledge and expression, of liberation and human kindness, of mutuality and connection, of communitarian, non-competitive aspirations. But on the days I want to teach like my colleagues I don't feel the outrage of the pious. More accurately, I feel like a rabbit looking for a safe hole to hide in until the semester has blown by. Inevitably though, the fantasy stagnates and instead I show up, slightly illegitimate, different from the guys in suits—again.

Sore Thumbs

Even if I was not to present a course in the feminist traditions of participatory learning and context-based ethics, I would be an oddity at Creighton if
for no other reason than I am a woman. The demographics where I work are a
powerful reminder of my difference. Being a woman, let alone a feminist, in this
medical school sets me aside because there are only a very few women here. At
receptions and faculty meetings, women seek each other out in the corners, a
tiny group finding support and company in a sea of men.

There are no women deans or department chairs in the Creighton School
of Medicine. I am the only woman course director for the students' first two
years of medical training. MIs and MIIs have exposure to several other women
during those years as lecturers in other classes; all but a few of these women lecture either in the Behavioral Science or Ethics and Health Policy courses. But
for their first two years, I am the only woman who structures the class content,
selects learning materials, and designs their assignments and exams. Perhaps
most significant from the students' point of view is that I am the only woman
who gives them a grade.

"Sticking out like a sore thumb" seems an unattractive, painful image to
describe my experience of being a woman in this position. But it may have
some validity given the gender ratio at Creighton. Like the feminist high school
teachers described by Kathleen Weiler, I am almost always conscious of myself
as a woman at the medical center (Weiler 1988). This consciousness is partially voluntary and partially a function of how others see me. Even before
opening my mouth here, I am preceded by my reputation as a feminist.

What is it about me that shows? I now take seriously my responsibility to
be a role model, even in a context where students, colleagues, and administrators vary in their attitude toward feminism from hostile to respectful. I think
about my demeanor with students, colleagues, and administrators, hoping to
project an image of a woman who doesn't make distinctions between her personal and professional selves.

I do not believe I have experienced discrimination from being labeled a
feminist. My tenure case was approved unanimously and I am not excluded
from committees and official functions of the school. But what is uncomfortable
is the sense of being an outsider, someone who is smart but somewhat weird all
the same. Someone who is not like the others. Partly this is because I am not a
physician. As a social scientist teaching ethics and health policy I will always feel
and always be on the margins of the medical school. However, gender also
contributes to the experience of institutional alienation.

Deborah Tannen writes that all women in settings dominated by men
carry a reputation regardless of how we chose to present ourselves. We are
"marked," in her linguistic terms, and there is no way around it in current

society (Tannen 1993). I am convinced it is better to be known as a feminist than as not, regardless of what the term connotes. But what is disturbing is how little actual control I have over how I will be read, what sources of information about myself are being attributed to the label, or most importantly, what meaning is given to it.

Recently my friend Judy recalled when I phoned her several years ago, near tears about a teaching evaluation from a student who wrote that I was "too feminist." Looking for support, I asked her, "What did "too feminist" mean anyway? How could I not be a feminist when that defines such an essential piece of my identity and moral character?"

Two things are significant about the phone call for this examination of feminism in medical education. First, the fact that I was so affected by a student's evaluation separates me from many of my male colleagues. I try not to care so much what the students think of me or the class. But I do. My socialization, not unlike other women in this society, has made it difficult and ultimately undesirable to compartmentalize my self from my work. Thus, not liking my *class* means not liking *me*. Furthermore, the relational base of the pedagogy I use requires a certain sense of connectedness with the students and consequently, vulnerability.

Second, I felt attacked by the student's comment for being what I could never not be or would never not want to be. But still, I confess to feeling shame for being something the student did not like. Shame, I wonder? Shame that I was not what he (or anyone else to whom I would give my authority) wanted me to be. Or fear? At one time I thought the fear evoked from such accusations was for my physical safety and job security, but I now understand the real fear is that I might betray myself to fit their agenda by showing up, as it were, in a man's ill-fitting suit. I felt both shame and fear on this occasion, until with my friend's support I recovered enough to say, "Good, he got it. I'm getting through with my advocacy, and it is causing them to reflect critically."

I must be gaining confidence in this opinion because this year I felt only gleeful pride when a faculty member levelled the same criticism at me and another colleague for our role on the Institutional Review Board. He wrote to the university president complaining about the obstructive values and interests represented by the "radical feminists" on the board. Although I was not shown the letter, we think he objected to our systematic questions about the exclusion of women from protocols and irrelevant HIV testing of research subjects.

Friends here call it the "F-word." Feminist is not an esteemed label in Omaha, especially among many students. I still feel regret about causing a woman medical student to be embarrassed when I first arrived from Berkeley to teach at Creighton. In a discussion of an ethics case I linked her opinion of empathetic behavior to the feminist concept of an ethics of care. Unaware of the extent of stigma attached to the term feminist, my intention had been to validate her voice by drawing on a respected tradition of ethical analysis. Instead, her fellow students hissed and mocked her for this association with feminism. I learned that it is one thing to stand as a feminist myself and thus assert my definition of the term through my behavior and words; to paraphrase Gloria Steinem, "This is what a feminist looks like." But I know better now than to use the term in reference to another, especially someone who could be hurt by the attribution.

This is what one feminist looks like

This essay challenges me to think about what I do mean by the label of feminist. I know I am one, but what does that mean to me? I think it has to do with differences. And that the differences that women bring, which I believe to be more by virtue of nurture than nature, are important contributions to our society. But feminism is also about equality. No contradiction in this for an anthropologist. As a profession we are dedicated to preserving the rich heterogeneity of social life while at the same time working towards more equitable distribution of wealth and power for *all* people. Can't have one without the other.

I have been influenced by the work of Carol Gilligan (1982), Sara Ruddick (1989), Sandra Harding (1991), and other cultural feminists writing about feminist ethics and epistemologies. After many years of academic training in patriarchal theories and pedagogies, it has been such a relief to come "home" to the sense that my intuitive/socialized competencies in teaching and scholarship are intellectually legitimate. To be a feminist in this sense is to embrace contradiction, to think consistency is a small-minded goal for intellectual thought, and to encompass much more than linear rationality in our analyses of reality. Dreams, poetry, and the messy emotionality of relationships also have relevance, as do our critiques of misused power, authority, and dominance.

For me being a feminist also means that I share a vocabulary of outrage at injustice and inequity based on gender, class, sexual orientation, and ethnic identity. My conception of feminism (recognizing its multiple meanings) does not discredit men or their contributions to our way of life necessarily, but I insist that women's ways of knowing and relating must also influence the organization of knowledge and social life where we work, learn, play, govern, raise children, heal the sick, bury the dead, sanction the wrong-doers, etc. I openly scorn the tendencies socialized in males to trample others, deny others a place at the table, and play dog games of hierarchy and who's on top. The values of efficiency and order are to be ridiculed and challenged when they are gained at the expense of generativity, compassion, and participatory decision-making. In the medical academy in particular I look forward to feminist administrators who are more likely to think in metaphors of webs rather than pyramids (Ferguson 1984).

The Need for Support

Although I may never find (or want) a fit within the formal structures of the medical school, given that it remains a conservative bastion of reductionism and bureaucratic dominance, I have been fortunate to find much support for my style of feminism elsewhere. Part of this fortune derives from the anomaly of academic traditions allowing for a kind of intellectual autonomy unique to the working world. Contrary to my initial fears about Creighton's Jesuit heritage, the university's commitment to academic freedom translates into a wide and worldly latitude of research, teaching, and community service—encompassing even feminist ideology and practice.

I have found comfort and intellectual stimulation from several feminist groups on and off campus that I helped to form. For example, once a month about ten women from different university departments meet as the Women's Research Seminar, a euphemism for an unstructured discussion of feminist scholarship in theology, sociology, anthropology, psychology, and philosophy. Our discussions blend insights about a chosen reading with our experience as feminist educators, researchers, and activists. These lunch meetings are a refuge, a place where trusted friends gather in support of our personal and professional development. Unfortunately, none of the women medical faculty I have invited have been able to attend our meetings. Increasingly, the pressure to see patients has made even teaching seem like an academic luxury for clinical faculty. As a faculty member who volunteers for my course told her peers at a curriculum meeting, "Taking time to lead a group discussion in Kate Brown's class is like sneaking out for a cigarette on the backstairs in high school. Just hope the practice manager doesn't catch you!" Medical students experience similar crunches, leaving little time or energy for such organized women-centered activities as the Center for Health Policy and Ethics' annual Women and Health Lecture sponsored by a consortium of campus and community women's groups or AMWA meetings.

This situation is more than unfortunate. Seeing the value of group support and taking time for it are essential for change to occur in medical education. When women remain isolated from each other it is difficult for us to differentiate institutional from personal sources of impotence and alienation. It remains easier to blame ourselves for what is not rightly ours. And without support we shy away from proposing changes that would more closely reflect the gifts we have to bring as women to health care education, organization, and delivery. Generative affiliations can create islands of support where we share assumptions, let the guard down for a time, and where, consequently, we can find the courage to wear the suit that fits.

CHAPTER 10

Feminist Criticism in Literature and Medicine

◻

Delese Wear

"We always 'see' from points of view that are invested with our social, political and personal interests, inescapably 'centric' in one way or another, even in the desire to do justice to heterogeneity."

—Susan Bordo (1990, 140)

At a recent annual meeting of those who teach humanities in medical settings, I was seated in a large room listening to a well-known and highly-regarded ethicist when, as an aside, he spoke of a "quick Rawls read." Most of the audience—white, middle-class, well-educated—politely laughed, connected to each other with a coded familiarity that enabled us to participate in the so-called Great Conversation. At that moment we were engaged in a rather harmless form of academic posturing, if we didn't consider those in the audience unfamiliar with Rawls who felt a bit illiterate. OK, I said to myself as I tried to diminish the effect of his words, it's just one offhand remark in the midst of a large meeting, not deeply symbolic of some larger, systemic design. But I heard very little of the remaining paper.

It's happening, I thought. The medical humanities, which emerged several decades ago as an outsider discourse in its relationship to medicine, seem to be almost assimilated into medicine, rather than hovering around its borders. The magnetic, persuasive power of medicine has transformed the medical humanities into one more academic department in the directory on the wall, with tight security at the borders of the knowledge in each discipline represented. This, of course, is probably viewed with satisfaction by some. But from where I'm situated, this assimilation has slowly distorted and now seeks to control the nature and purpose of our work. No longer on the outside, humanities inquiry in medicine has ceased to be unruly, confrontive, and daring. In the past such inquiry would unravel rather than connect, agitate rather than steady, disturb rather than reassure.

103

I've been thinking about this transformation a great deal lately as I listen to my colleagues at meetings and read their essays in journals. I wonder how a "quick Rawls read" is translated back home in our classes of medical students and residents who are struggling to make meaning of their medicalized lives, and how it symbolizes much of the scholarly activity in the medical humanities. But mostly, I'm troubled as I reflect on my *own* teaching, trying to find meaning and purpose in this still-strange land of literature and medicine. I believe that humanities inquiry—literature in particular—can confront, critique, and unsettle learners. With that as a goal, my literature classes should be sites of uneasiness, of exploding preconceptions, of self-conscious examinations of values and beliefs. My classes should be sites of resistance from the taken-for-granted, a place where our thinking and actions are under scrutiny, where we can directly challenge the sexism, racism, classism, and heterosexism in ourselves, our culture, and in the practice of medicine.

One way to move literary inquiry in medical education in this direction is to ground it theoretically in feminist criticism, which views any knowledge as inadequate that censures or ignores the experiences, perspectives, and persons of most of the human race (Messer-Davidow 1989). Feminist criticism is, of course, tied to the larger sociopolitical movement of feminism, which resists not only the subjugation of women but is also committed to countering oppression of all people.* Thus, feminism's connection to medical practice in general, medicine and literature in particular, is as follows: if honoring the multiplicity and diversity of human experience is a goal of a just and caring medical practice, then examining and challenging *any* oppressive custom that undermines such caregiving should be one of the primary goals of literary inquiry in medical settings.

How might all this fit into our current practice of teaching literature and medicine? This is difficult to answer; our teaching is diverse because we who teach literature and medicine are a diverse group. But it is safe to say that feminist criticism in literature and medicine is not silent about any oppressive practice in medicine in both the physical and fictional world. Feminist criticism does not tiptoe or whisper, it does not automatically mimic scientific/medical epistemologies, nor does it look unproblematically at the emerging medicine and literature canon. Rather, it is often interested in working quite literally from the outside, going no further "in" than the borders between literature and medicine, resisting the pull to enter the inner cir-

---

*I realize how richly ambiguous the term feminism is. Because there is no monolithic definition of feminism, it is inherently plural even though throughout this essay I use it in the singular. For here, I focus on what the various feminisms have in common, that is, a deep commitment to eliminate oppression of women, and to work in the struggle against other unjust power relations based on race, ethnicity, social class, sexual orientation, and so on.

cle of medicine as the only site of legitimacy or sanction.

Further, feminist criticism is not indiscriminate regarding competing narratives in literature and medicine. In fact, it refuses to "uncritically link explanatory frames without making visible the contesting assumptions on which they are often premised . . . [it makes explicit] the ways the production of the social real in language shapes and is in turn shaped by divisions of labor and formations of state . . . as well as . . . the ways meaning is the effect of social struggle" (Hennessy 1993, 15). When viewed this way, feminist criticism is a "mode of praxis . . . [its] point is to change the world" (Schweickart 1986, 38). Confronting morally unacceptable medical practices, then, would be one reflection of a feminist presence in literature and medicine.

Thus, I posit that feminist criticism become one alternative framework for teaching literature in medical settings, whereby issues illuminated by literature take readers deeper into the personal and political domains, where teachers and students together engage in critically questioning exclusionary or oppressive practices, norms, or standards, overt or subtly enacted, in both the culture at large and in the medical culture that reflects those practices. Such a framework is not based on medicine- or canon-bashing, or on dismissing all Western philosophical traditions. Rather, this feminist in particular often and gleefully uses works found predictably on many literature and medicine syllabi, and insists on close, analytical readings of the texts I assign. I find traditional works important not because they represent eternal truths but because students can benefit from reading the works of such visionaries,

> to show them how to think, to teach them how to keep their minds open. And that is also the reason we need to include new voices in the curriculum—to show all students that they can participate, as thinkers, readers, writers, and critics, in the cultivation of new classics. The best way to honor our traditions is to extend them. (Beverly and Fox 1989, 52)

As I reflect on many of the ideas suggested here, I have come to believe that any teaching in the medical academy informed by feminism may move us and our students to think about the taken-for-granted in classes, corridors and conferences rooms; in relationships with patients; and within the institutions where we do our work. In that respect, feminism can provide one theoretical position (among others) for those in academic medicine willing to engage in a reflective, ongoing critique of medical practice in our culture. But in the following paragraphs I will narrow the discussion to how feminist criticism may confront and perhaps influence our thought and practice as we teach and talk about literature and medicine. I begin by telling a story about a literature and medicine class I teach, then step back to reflect on and critique the teaching and curriculum issues raised by this classroom episode.

I was to begin a new class in a few days. In addition to rereading the literature I'd assigned, I spent a great deal of time thinking about what I was going to say during that introductory class. The goal of the class, "Women's Health Issues in Literature," was to examine how selected literature works to portray major health events in most women's lives; how race, class, and sexual orientation may influence the experience of illness and the delivery of care; and how these literary depictions might deepen and enlarge students' perceptions of these issues and possibly compel them to work at oppositional and transformative angles to unjust social relations in medicine.

But there was much, much more going on here for me than merely preparing for class. I wanted to make explicit from the beginning what the roaming, murmuring background was in all my classes, a background that was clearly feminist. I wanted this class to be a place to confront racism, sexism, classism, heterosexism, and other oppressive beliefs and acts in ourselves; in students' relationships with patients; in medical education (including this class); in hospitals and clinics. When I named myself feminist at the onset, I hoped to explain how that position might influence what went on in class. I wanted to do so not as some act of bravado, or to focus attention on myself in a kind of solipsistic teacher confessional or testimonial. Rather, I wanted to establish an atmosphere with my students that would focus our thinking and our relationships with one another and with patients in a way that might call into question prescribed, medicalized postures of authoritative and categorical thought. Of course, I thought I had worked toward this during my years of teaching literature and medicine. Yet, as I uneasily reflected back on this teaching, I wasn't so sure.

With all this in mind, I began the new class. I told students how the class had been simmering for several years as I became more aware of the disparities between clinical accounts of women's health issues, and women's lived accounts of these experiences, often startlingly portrayed in fiction. I disclosed how my feminism fueled what I saw, heard, and read in my medical surroundings. I detailed how literature could be studied as it focused attention on the following: cultural inequities; where we stood in relation to oppressive beliefs and acts; what we were willing to do regarding oppressiveness we enacted and witnessed; what all this might mean in the larger medical system that perpetrated differential treatment based on race, gender, sexual orientation, and ability to pay. I also revealed my worries, how I might unknowingly silence or shame students who did not share my explicit zealotry. I told them how I feared I could be enacting in less overt form what any number of intolerant clinicians or professors demanded daily on teaching rounds in hospitals. I revealed that we would be talking often about what was going on in class, and I earnestly invited them to speculate how my professorial privilege would interfere with honest self-disclosure on their part regarding a subject so obviously critical to me. Many students nodded, all were silent, most looked uneasy or a bit embarrassed at this monologue. I was uneasy too, so we moved on into discussion of the literature I'd assigned for this class.

The topics were birth, abortion, miscarriage, and infertility. We read and discussed poetry by Linda Pastan, Lucille Clifton, and Sharon Olds, and a short story by Margaret Atwood. We searched for meanings in the language of fiction to tell the stories differently from clinical accounts and conventional knowledge of medicine: what did this woman think when she looked down in the toilet and saw the remnants of her pregnancy: "clots of blood . . . Dark red like black in the salty / translucent brine" (Olds 1984, 25)? Or, what about this mother's cynical description of a contemporary United States delivery room, where she was "strapped down / victim in an old comic book" (Pastan 1982, 26)? A spirited discussion surrounded these poems, and I, the only non-medical person in the room, became voyeur once again through my students' accounts of what they see daily in hospitals.

But then the difficulties began. We read aloud an excerpt from Toni Morrison's novel, *The Bluest Eye* (1970), written in the voice of a black woman, Pauline, who decides to go to the hospital to have her second child rather than have it at home as she did with her first. While the story takes place over fifty years ago, we still cringed at the cruel overtness of the racist male doctor who, at Pauline's bedside, remarks casually to the young doctors rounding with him, "These here women you don't have any trouble with. They deliver right away and with no pain. Just like horses" (99). Only one of the younger doctors looked at Pauline's face, and when he did, she knew that he was ashamed at what he had just witnessed. He knew, Pauline thought, that she was no mare foaling, but he didn't respond and moved on with the rest of them as they begin examining a white woman nearby, fussing over her, asking her how she was doing. Pauline's pains get worse, and she starts moaning "something awful" even though the pains aren't as bad as she is letting on. But she needs to let everyone know that

> I hurt just like them white women. Just 'cause I wasn't hooping and hollering before didn't mean I wasn't feeling pain. What'd they think? That just 'cause I knowed how to have a baby with no fuss that my behind wasn't pulling and aching like theirs? (99)

One young woman, a fourth-year student, started to describe her experiences during her obstetrics/gynecology rotation. Much of her training during this rotation (currently true for many medical students in the United States) had been in ob/gyn clinics in hospitals. Her remarks turned the discussion away from Pauline to herself, even as she continued to speak on the subject of oppression. As the discussion unfolded and other students joined in, I learned the pejorative way "clinic patient" or "house patient" was often used: Poor women/girls. Mostly black. Frequent drug/alcohol involvement. Multiple births. Noncompliant. Many with an "attitude." Few remarks commingled these *characterizations* of clinic patients with the *oppression* of clinic patients in terms of access, silencing, and other acts of medical marginalization.

Then more descriptions, more representations without students' concomitant acknowledgement of *their* part in the domination of these patients: "I lost count of how many pregnant fifteen-year-olds I saw who already had children"; "Clinic patients are less compliant"; "Clinic patients wait too long to get medical care." Then students' self-disclosures: "I was jaded within a week"; "It's hard to feel compassion for them"; or "I have to make myself go in there and try to give them the same care I would give to the CEO's wife, but it's tough."

I was speechless. I heard students revealing some very intimate feelings that deeply affected their roles and responsibilities as physicians. This was, after all, *part* of what I had hoped for all along: for us to identify oppressions, to see ourselves as victims *and* perpetrators of oppressions, and to come to a point where we were able to confront and oppose those oppressions? But many of these young doctors, *now in the trenches* taking care of people whose lives are broken and covered with the fallout of a culture that denigrates and ignores their very existence, viewed these clinic patients clearly as Other. They felt empathy for Pauline when they were reading and discussing the story, but did not make a link between Pauline and their own patients, or between Pauline's doctor(s) and their own doctoring. Still, I said very little, and as the class ended, I was baffled and frustrated. It took me days of thinking and talking with several colleagues to identify the obvious. I realized that in the clinical scenarios they provided in response to *The Bluest Eye*, students identified *themselves* as the victims, put in situations where they felt unprepared and overwhelmed, confronted with humans whose lives were alien to what most of them had ever experienced. In their frustration, exasperation, and inability to understand, *they* were the exploited ones in a medical system that sloughed off care of the poor to medical students, who were themselves at the bottom of the heap in the care-giving hierarchy. Not quite a kick-the-dog phenomenon, but in the same family of response.

The various feminisms, regardless of their particular orientations, are deeply committed to exposing and articulating the gendered nature of history, culture, and society. As a teacher who admits vulnerability and uncertainty in my teaching and writing, I struggle daily with what it means to bring my convictions openly into my classes and my relationships with students and colleagues. This is difficult to do, to name one's deeply felt commitments while guarding against pontification and encouraging a kind of group-think based on correct answers—an educative scenario that replaces one pattern of domination with the tyranny of political correctness.

Sandra Harding is helpful here when she distinguishes between the "coercive values" of racism, classism, and sexism that distort and mystify our culture's explanations and understandings of difference; and the "participatory values" of anti-racism, anti-classism, anti-sexism that honor, with authenticity and without patronizing, the individual human life across all of our differences (quoted in Lather 1991, 3). Those of us who teach literature and medicine, making explicit our commitment to participatory values, must still be vigilant about the necessity of self-reflexivity, of examining how our presence permeates our classes in ways we might not intend, of discovering how we can be in collusion with that which we critique in medicine when we replace poses of objectivity with overt politics (Lather, 10). Thus, being open about our convictions as we teach mandates critical self-examination of that very teaching, making it impossible for us to recede behind the content we teach and the methods we use in our teaching.

As the preceding classroom scenario indicates, I am engaged in this kind of continuing, reflective, often difficult critique of my teaching. Focusing back on the women students in class, I try to understand how they have been rewarded for passivity and indoctrinated in stereotypical sex roles in all of their educational experiences. I try to identify my complicity as a teacher in promoting a sexist, racist, classist, heterosexist education. I look at the daily examples of our lives as teachers, doctors, and administrators in patriarchical settings (medical schools, hospitals, medical practices), and how this informs students and residents about our values and beliefs. I scrutinize our actions with women students in formal and informal situations, not merely our overt and subtle exchanges with them but even how we listen to them.

Yes, I have been looking for ways to help my students and me confront how all of us are victims and perpetrators of various human abuses, yet we have looked too little at our own complicity in cultural/medical power plays. In the class I described, the women students did identify oppression, but only others' enactment of it in the huge medical/cultural system of hierarchies and power, stopping short of identifying their fit in the rest of the chain of domination where they unwittingly oppressed other women. But the difference in the degree and kind of oppression women students experience and that of their women patients is obvious, in addition to the fact that women students know they will not be in their present place forever. Theirs was a resistance of silence and compliance to survive, to get out of the system to enter it again, the next time with the power they now lacked.

Lewis and Simon remind us that "oppression is enacted not by theoretical concepts but by real people in concrete situations" (1986, 469): on teaching rounds, in literature and medicine classes, in lectures and informal exchanges, and elsewhere. Students described their own oppressive behavior that was not as overt as Pauline's physician's racism, yet they were unable or unwilling to examine how the subtle differences in care they give to clinic patients—perhaps unaware and unintentional—were one more predictable, relentless enactment of power and privilege leveled against the disenfranchised.

But how to see these roles of victim and oppressor as intricately mixed? Although matter-of-fact about the inequities and injustices in their own medical education and in the clinical scenarios they witnessed and took part in every day, these medical students were still troubled and confused. Contrary to much current popular cynicism about doctors, I find medical students entering medicine full of energetic, altruistic idealism. As the realities of power and authority become routinized in their education, their will to survive the moment often transcends their social conscience; they are more like the young doctor who looks at Pauline's face, silently knowing yet moving on. And often it takes reading Pauline's story to remind students of what is behind the gazes of many of their patients.

Yes, it is true that in this particular class, Pauline did little more than trigger students' disclosures of life in the clinic. What *they* chose to identify as oppression—their own—was compelling and immediate. Their examination was quite above ground in a matter-of-fact blaming mode, never venturing below to their own enactment of power and oppression (where Professor wanted them to go). Still, I believe that literature, with its rich, unsettling ambiguities, can be a place to launch a critique of dominant positionings *if* we are able to examine—partial and biased as that examination will be—what lies below the murky surface of our teaching and doctoring. But in the midst of that discussion, I did not know how to venture there with students; I was too caught up in my position that kept me in my clean, antiseptic classroom, where I was clearly *not* the one touching and probing the bodies and minds of persons so different from me in clinics all across the city as students are required to do. Moreover, my commitments *not* to engage in "you should/you shouldn't" with students, *not* to posture as the one with answers, washed away and lost a critical moment in our class when a reflective, self-conscious critique of our beliefs and practice should have occurred.

Yet it is within these concrete situations that we as teachers can alter our postures that result in a discourse that *appears* objective and distanced; a single discourse that proclaims to be the locus of certainty, certification, legitimation; a discourse that is ultimately a vehicle for domination as we (clasping our disciplines/"expertise") pose as those who know what "they"—students and the marginalized they care for—need and want. Physician David Hilfiker talks of physicians confronting their own brokenness as they care for their very broken patients: "We need to bring ourselves more into the process of healing, not just our expertise . . . doctors need to know how to really be able to feel their patients' pain. And the only way to be able to feel a patient's pain is by being willing to face your own" (1989, 96-97). Perhaps that is where Pauline and others like her can help us uncover not only the pain of patients, but our own pain. This is where I must learn to go with students, a place that is near *but is not the same as* their feelings of victimization by the medical system. Identifying their victimization is essential, and to gather enough courage to confront the medicalized system of domination would be an extraordinary measure, especially if it is enacted in multiple voices. But to leave out of that confrontation the difficult and puzzling recognition of the ways we/they dominate and oppress patients is to deny one of the many potentials for literary inquiry in medicine. My challenge was how to tie the unaffected, evocative immediacy of Pauline's experience (that students empathically identified with) to the clinic patients.

In the preceding pages, I have maintained that those of us who teach literature and medicine are not mandated to "expose" our students to the selected tradition in literature and medicine. Instead, my proposition has been that we select and read literature that (1) portrays lives and experiences both inside and outside dominant cultural perspectives; (2) causes us to reflect on our own active or passive role in reinforcing practices that reject, ignore, or openly hurt others within a culture grounded in racism, sexism, heterosexism, classism, and other oppressive beliefs; (3) may prompt us to change, to work in the service of the feminist commitment to end the exploitation and oppression of all humans.

Everything on which these beliefs rests is based on a premise that has, I hope, been an implicit thread weaving its way throughout this essay: that literature has the power to make things happen, that it can help us to "think beyond our limits, while acknowledging limits" (Tillman 1991, 102). Reading literature in medical settings may inspire us to examine our unspoken beliefs, to do what we never thought about doing, to do what we must to provide care that *is* caring and inclusive. It has to do with Maxine Greene's image of what education might be on any level, in any domain,

> conceived as a process of futuring, of releasing persons to become different, of provoking persons to repair lacks and to take action to create themselves . . . This means that one's "reality," rather than being fixed and predefined, is a perpetual emergent, becoming increasingly multiplex, as more perspectives are taken, more texts are opened . . . [it is] a vision of education that brings together the need for wide-awakeness with the hunger for community. (1988, 22-23)

This image is possible even in medical settings if we, too, think about what we're doing when we teach literature and medicine—why we teach, how we teach, what we teach.

As I look back to where I started, I offer the following scenario. I am seated in a large room at a conference with my colleagues who teach humanities in medical settings. A well-known and highly respected ethicist, a woman, has just given an aside, suggesting that we do a "quick Kristeva read." The audience laughs politely, because they, like the speaker, are well-grounded in outsider discourses; they know Rawls, yes, but they also think of philosophy (and literature, and science, and other provinces of knowing) as disciplines that are informed by perspectives far more inclusive than those predictable ones we've all been provided in the academy. And while she is up there talking, she is telling us about her teaching and theorizing in a consciously first-person autobiographical stance. She is engaged in a "willing, knowledgeable, outspoken involvement . . . with the subject matter" and extends to her listeners (and her students) an invitation to "participate in the interweaving and construction of the ongoing conversation." (Miller 1991, 24)

Yes, there is still posturing going on here, but each time we redraw or enlarge the boundaries of our knowing, richer, more abundant, more imaginative thinking is likely to occur. I sketch this scenario not to replace little boy philosophers chuckling with one another about Rawls with little girl feminist critics chuckling with one another about Kristeva. I envision this because I do not live and teach in a vacuum. I have deep regard for my colleagues, my peers, their scholarship, their thinking. I think, learn, study, read, and teach, not just in my twentieth century educated Western web, but in the smaller intellectual community of these scholars and teachers of the medical humanities. Our discourse is important to me, but I want the discourse to be more inclusive, just as I want my teaching to be more inclusive of persons underrepresented, forgotten, or ignored by the culture that informs current medical practice. Maxine Greene concludes,

> This may be, in the last analysis, what seems to connect artistry and teaching—this effort to open out of the commonplace, out of the cotton wool of habit and dailyness, to discover (in our plurality, in our human being together) what it is like to look at things as if they could be otherwise and somehow learn enough to actualize that otherwise in decency—and then to move beyond. (1987, 9)

CHAPTER 11

Innovations in Residency Education:
General Internal Medicine–Women's Health Residency Track

❑

Pamela Charney

How did I get here?

Fortunately, my early fascination with science was fostered by my parents. I was often reminded of other women in science including those in our extended family. Throughout my education, I continued to be interested in scientific knowledge and research. Medicine became a career choice through conversations with my father, who articulated for me the enthusiasm and pleasure I had relating to people as well as studying science. My college advisor also encouraged my interest in medicine as a career where my interest in interdisciplinary perspectives could be nurtured.

Once I was in medical training, I found internal medicine a discipline committed to the challenge of making connections, de-mystifying health and disease, and managing complex illness. Internists considered the whole patient, which included her occupation, family, environment, and community. The primary care internists went one step further and expanded knowledge into other disciplines; this is where I found my home. For me, being a real doctor means lifelong learning, teamwork with patients and their families, and focusing on interdisciplinary collaboration.

I completed an internal medicine residency and a one year fellowship in general medicine to learn more about home visits, elderly housing programs, dermatology, gynecology, sports medicine, substance abuse, ENT and psychiatry. After all this training, I was eager to provide direct care to a diverse patient population. When I joined a Health Maintenance Organization practice, I soon found that I needed additional skills in gynecology, breast care, and medical care of the surgical patient. I learned from a variety of sources, including consulting physicians for my patients, as well as time spent in the library.

I also found myself expanding more at interfaces with other disciplines, first obstetrics and gynecology, and then psychiatry. When an overweight

113

woman in my practice developed gestational diabetes, I discussed the management of her care with a perinatologist and obstetrician. Soon, I found myself volunteered to care for other pregnant diabetic patients and diabetic woman considering pregnancy. Working closely with women highly motivated to improve diabetic control put pregnancy in a different perspective.

Subsequently I had a similar experience in psychiatry. One day while seeing a patient who had acute medical problems, I met a very manic woman who had been on Lithium for years. She not only had pressured speech, but also had large, almost wild eyes with lid lag, sweaty palms, and tachycardia. When I diagnosed and treated her overactive thyroid, her psychiatric problem only minimally improved, so she was still seen weekly in the psychiatry department. Soon many other psychiatrically ill patients decided to see if I could find out what else might be wrong. Some had medical problems that had been missed, and many had symptoms that I could not diagnose. Later when the department of psychiatry decided to develop an alcohol abuse evaluation and treatment unit within the department of medicine, I was recruited, and agreed to serve without title, raise, or administrative time. But I learned an enormous amount about substance abuse, and in my own practice I began to ask more effective questions and was able to diagnose patients earlier in the course of their disease.

When I returned to New York City and academics to teach, I settled at a medical center that provides care for many immigrants and underserved patients, and where their Primary Care Internal Medicine Residency is committed to expanding resident skills beyond those in more traditional internal medicine. For example, I was encouraged to develop a course on peri-operative care, working closely with surgeons and anesthesiologists. The High Risk Maternity Clinic was supported by attendings from both obstetrics and medicine to maximize the care of the medically ill pregnant patient. All this is to say that I was delighted to be at an institution where I was free to work at clinical interfaces.

Then and now my clinical practice serves ethnically and financially diverse patients ranging in age from eighteen to old age. I care for many first generation immigrants, and I am honored to care for several multigenerational families, clusters of friends, and neighbors. Together with my patients and their families, I work to maintain health and control acute and chronic medical problems.

Soon after arriving in New York, I also began to collaborate with other feminist educators in medical education by joining the Women's Caucus of the Society of General Internal Medicine. The group had begun a critical review of the large clinical trials used as a rationale for the treatment of hypertension, often over pot luck dinners where we discussed medical literature. It became evident how seldom research design included gender as an independent variable. Yet we knew that including women subjects without exploring gender differences can lead to assumptions that may not be correct.

When I suggested at the end of one of our presentations of our findings that this was the tip of the iceberg, someone in the audience challenged me to prove it. Within a few years I began collaborating with Dr. Carole Morgan. We reviewed the 1990 *Annals of Internal Medicine, Journal of the American Medical Association*, and the *New England Journal of Medicine* to identify all treatment trials. For each trial, we determined patient gender, whether there was any evidence of data analysis by gender, and whether treatment recommendations were gender neutral. We discovered that if two large follow up studies of men were excluded (the Doctor's aspirin study and a Mr. FIT follow-up), then 40% of the subject pool were women, but only 14% of the studies including women and men had any evidence of data analysis by gender, and almost all treatment recommendations were gender neutral. Our current research is comparing 1990 and 1994 treatment trials.

It is within this context of my practice, teaching, and research that I found a new professional adventure, one in which I can direct my general commitment to medicine *and* my focused interest in women's health: the creation of a General Internal Medicine-Women's Health Residency Tract. The remainder of this chapter provides a rationale for the residency, development of clinical and educational experiences, and a description of faculty critical to its success.

Rationale

When we talk about women's health, we include the full spectrum of women's experiences, and look to other disciplines to inform our understanding of gender's influence on health. That is, in addition to medical and other health disciplines, physiology, psychology, and sociology can also add to our understandings. Thus, women's health is substantially more than the study of sexual hormones and reproductive health.

Most clinicians have deferred exploring interdisciplinary knowledge relating to women's health until after completing medical training. Only a small number of specialties, such as obstetrics and gynecology, have included a focus on gender and health issues as part of the educational process. Individual clinicians in other specialties who are interested in gender and health issues have been largely self and peer educated. But as more clinicians and specialties become interested in gender, efforts to integrate cross-disciplinary knowledge and skills become more available and successful.

In the 1990s, several trends are intersecting which will transform medical and residency education to consider gender issues in greater depth. First, the number of women practicing and teaching medicine has increased. Second, the body of medical knowledge about gender and health has begun to explode. Third, public interest about gender differences and similarities is high. As a consequence of these factors, there is an increasing acceptance among health professionals of the importance of considering gender in health and disease.

Departments of internal medicine have been variable in their attention to the importance of gender in providing patient care, educating housestaff and students, mentoring at all levels, and recruiting and promoting faculty. But recently, some departments of internal medicine have developed special educational programs such as a women's health lecture series, journal clubs focused on women's health, and various support groups. But the General Internal Medicine–Women's Health Track at the Albert Einstein College of Medicine and Bronx Municipal Hospital Center is a more comprehensive effort to integrate women's health concerns into the discipline of internal medicine.

Development

The idea to create a women's health track in an internal medicine residency occurred to Dr. Robert Meyer, Director of Medicine at Bronx Municipal Hospital Center, while he was walking past one of the hospitals that had been originally constructed as a tuberculosis sanitorium. On the front of the building hangs a large sculpture of a man, woman and child. As a general internist with special expertise in pharmacology, Dr. Meyer contemplated how little we still know about women. Creating a new program with a focus on women's health could speed up the process by which physicians develop and integrate new insights about gender and health. Because of my background and interests, I was asked to create this new program, which is still in its evolutionary phase.

The General Internal Medicine–Women's Health Track is being developed in institutions that have prided themselves in interdisciplinary collaboration. The long relationship between the department of medicine and the department of obstetrics and gynecology at the Albert Einstein College of Medicine has included a number of internists who hold joint appointments. While there are several established Primary Care Internal Medicine residencies at Einstein, none of them has developed the close collaboration with the department of obstetrics and gynecology planned for the General Internal Medicine–Women's Health Track.

Both the department of obstetrics and gynecology and the department of internal medicine have many of their academic staff based across the street from the medical school at the Jacobi Medical Center. This large public hospital facility is part of the Health and Hospitals Corporation of New York City. Its strength includes a diverse patient base that claims the hospital as its own, a core attending staff in multiple specialties committed to caring for all patients, a close relationship with the medical school, and effective hospital administration.

Residents in the General Internal Medicine–Women's Health Track will learn to provide excellent comprehensive care to both women and men patients. Comprehensive care includes first contact, continuity and coordination of care, and health promotion as well as care for acute and chronic health problems. General internists are often the specialists of the undifferentiated complaint, "It hurts there." To complete these tasks, it is essential to be able to communicate effectively with patients, their families, and other health professionals. It is also critical to understand and be able to respond to normal psychological challenges of life as well as psychopathology.

Educational activities include providing patient care in usual and innovative settings, classroom activities, mentorship by special faculty, and exposure to research. Residents will provide continuity care in both a primary care medical clinic and in the gynecology division of the Women's Health Center. The former will provide exposure to younger patients and common gynecologic problems, and will provide an opportunity to be a consultant about routine medical problems for gynecologic colleagues. These residents will be simultaneously supervised by attending physicians from both internal medicine and obstetrics and gynecology.

The core internal medicine faculty are practicing general internists based at the Jacobi Medical Center. Their responsibilities include providing continuity and interim care for a personal panel of patients, supervising students and residents in several clinical sites, and a variety of teaching and research activities. Many are internal medicine consultants to the High-Risk Maternity Clinic. Over the past several months, more classroom educational activities have been developed, such as the almost forty-hour course, "Gender and Coronary Artery Disease: Prevention, Diagnosis, and Management."

Faculty, Research, and Teaching Directions

Clinical and medical school faculty with a track record in gender and health issues are being approached individually to join the extended faculty of the General Internal Medicine–Women's Health track. The residents in this program will utilize these faculty as resources for improving clinical expertise or research projects. This diverse interdisciplinary faculty spans several hospitals and research centers, and includes both clinicians and researchers. The creation of the evening seminar series provides a regular forum for the extended faculty to come together.

My own bias is that too often gender and ethnicity are not considered when developing and interpreting intervention trials, yet results are reported as if they apply equally to everyone. The recent re-examination of coronary artery disease in women reflects the limitations of a gender blind approach. The importance of considering ethnicity and race is reinforced by literature on ethnicity and the incidence and natural history of renal failure, breast cancer, and violent deaths. Many other areas of physiology, and disease diagnosis and management are awaiting similar review and revision of our understanding.

The pharmacologic effects of many commonly used medications may be another frontier where gender may be particularly important. Too little is known of drug dosing, drug distribution, and drug side effects. The dose of medications may be an important variable when considering gender related outcomes. Almost all of the standard doses of medications in current use were determined by studies on young and middle-age white men, even in light of the fact that the distribution of many drugs is affected by the amount of water versus fat, and that body composition varies with gender and age. Focusing on race has also reveled potentially important differences in drug metabolism (e.g., Chinese men have greater sensitivity to propranolol than white men). There has also been inadequate research considering gender related adverse side effects. Finally, the implications of the higher compliance of women than men with medications and other medical recommendations await elucidation.

The evening seminar series explores some of these issues. Presentations are limited to twenty minutes to provide adequate opportunity for interdisciplinary discussion. In addition to faculty, these conferences are attended by residents from internal medicine, family practice, obstetrics and gynecology, pediatrics, psychiatry, and medical students. Topics planned for the start of the series include "What Is *Woman's* Health?," "Preconception Counseling," "Eating Disorders In Adolescence," and "Sex Hormones and Brain Function." Faculty, residents and students have been very enthusiastic about having a regular forum for exploration of gender and health issues.

The creation and development of a residency in General Internal Medicine-Women's Health Track provides new challenges. Together, with my colleagues, I hope to further explore the boundaries of our knowledge to improve the care women and men patients receive.

CHAPTER 12

Life as a Sheep in the Cow's Pasture

❑

Marian Gray Secundy

"Young lady, listen to me and get this straight once and for all. You are a sheep in a cow's pasture. You will always be a sheep in a cow's pasture. Get used to it. Accept it. Adapt or get out and go on about your life. Do you understand me? I am a sheep in a cow's pasture. There are limits to what I can do." My mentor, the Associate Dean of the medical school, handed me a tissue for my tear-stained face as she proceeded to repeat this speech to me over and over again. I had come in for perhaps the fourth or fifth time that month to complain about the disregard with which I was treated by the male chair of my department, about the consistent failure to get any of my ideas accepted, about the refusal of the entire system to change in appropriately creative ways, about the fact that not being a physician was bad enough in this medical school where I was the first medical humanities person ever hired, but being a woman was even worse. I had never before in my life confronted such openly chauvinistic, sexist, controlling men and here I was at five o'clock on a Tuesday afternoon being told by one of the most competent, brilliant women administrators I had ever met that we were only sheep in a cow's pasture and we had to accept that as the reality of our lives forever and ever, amen.

There are moments when a person knows that she is at a crossroads in her life. This was one of those moments. I knew I was being told something of vital importance to my future professional career. I knew I had to make a decision about if and how I was to go forward with the reality with which I had been presented or to pick up my marbles, toys, plans, dreams and go back to being a psychotherapist in a comfortable social work setting where women were in charge, where issues of disrespect and disregard did not surface. But because I had been taught from an early age that "a winner never quits and a quitter never wins," I would not. I could not be moved. Somehow I would find a way to get along. After all, my mentor had survived and despite being a sheep she was in fact the Associate Dean. And I *had* been able to get many of my ideas accepted: we now had elective courses in Managing Dying Patients and in Communication Skills, the first time ever that such courses had been taught in this medical school. The Dean, despite his concerns that the course about dying was "awfully morbid," had conceded that it probably should become a part of a required course for all entering students. Perhaps there was hope after all, at least for professional growth . . . but what, O Lord, was I going to do about the ways in which women were treated in this place? I began to ponder how I had ever reached this level of adulthood and not learned about the "proper role of women in the universe."

As the first-born child and daughter of very well-educated parents and grandparents (my father had a Ph.D., my mother a Master's degree, my maternal grandparents were college graduates), I had been brought up to believe I could do anything that I wanted, within, of course, the limits of what was possible for Negroes (as we were then called and called ourselves) in America. I had also been urged to prepare myself to be at the doors when those which were now closed were opened and I could walk through. We all knew, of course, that it was just a matter of time before they were opened because we were all prepared to push them open or hammer them down with our persistence, intelligence and skill. No one ever said in my house that men could or should be more prepared or push harder than women. I also attended an all female high school and college; thus, at critical times in my development I was in an environment in which there were no limits. On the other hand, there were definitely some contradictions. Assumptions of traditional female roles were expedited at both home and in other personal relations. My last conversation with my father before his death is forever proof of the importance of such traditions: he told me of his pride at my being a faculty member at Howard University but cautioned me to remember that I had to take care of my husband and children first.

Now I found myself in a male-dominated, physician-dominated medical school without the benefit of even a basic science degree, a place with no history or interest in social sciences, the humanities or assertive women who did not know their place, i.e. that they were indeed sheep in a cow's pasture. And each day someone did something or said something to remind me. I was forced to pay attention and to learn in painful ways that some of me would have to bend, or break. On the other hand there were major contradictions, for I was also in a predominantly black environment for the first time since grade school. The supportive nurturance for black people and their ideas and abilities were also here, even for non-physician women from the alien world of the social and behavioral sciences. Although my femaleness had never been a handicap in my high school or college, I had always carried my blackness as a challenge to the white teachers with whom I had contact. Yet even though I did not have one black teacher during high school or college, the teachers I did have were committed to learning more than they were to any notions of black inferiority. I was fortunate to have experienced the most accomplished of teachers in two very elite academic settings, The Philadelphia High School for Girls and Vassar College. Unlike bell hooks and many other blacks in white schools, I was unaware of having "to counter white racist assumptions that we were genetically inferior" (1994, 4). I expected to struggle with these issues and approached many of my teachers with a chip on my shoulder, but found them unwilling to engage at that level. Despite this good fortune, I still encountered racial tension at Vassar in the late 1950s, perhaps more in myself than in others, tension that I no longer felt at Howard University. I was simultaneously chained and unchained: free to experiment with the curriculum if I could overcome male authority . . . appropriately.

My conversation with Associate Dean Eleanor Franklin brought me face to face with certain harsh realities. Thank goodness I was in an historically black school and did not have to contend simultaneously with being a woman *and* being black, conditions that, I came to realize, present similar problems. Not having read any black feminist writers at the time, I thought I had come up with this brilliant insight all my own about the intersection of racism and sexism. I subsequently learned, of course, that black women writers and theorists speaking from feminist perspectives had already written eloquently about the similarities between the two and the coping mechanisms one chooses to deal with each. Yet despite the fact that I had learned successfully to negotiate being black in America, I was having one hell of a time negotiating being a woman in this medical school.

A variety of incidents come to mind, all which caused me to doubt myself and make me uncertain about my own responsibility for problems I had. Every expression of annoyance or anger was, and is today, termed female hysteria by many of my male colleagues. One doctor consistently threatens me with a shot of thorazine every time I complain about something. Anger is always translated as emotional instability. Any difficulty with another female secretary, colleague, or student is deemed a "woman thing," a personality conflict, never a real problem to be analyzed and handled. In one extraordinary encounter, a male colleague from the Middle East accused me of being rude and insubordinate for daring (his words) to disagree with him in front of others. He threatened to see that I "paid" for the indignity to his character. For years he made every effort to make good that threat and openly challenged, disagreed with, or criticized each and every input I made. Most recently, despite the fact that I had been elected as the faculty representative to the university's Board of Trustees in a university-wide election, I found a majority of my male colleagues supporting the candidacy of a male physician in an attempt to thwart my bid for re-election. My support came not from my own college and colleagues but from the majority of the university faculty in other schools and colleges. Although it was clear that the physician faculty would be much happier with one of their own in that position, I was re-elected. And I think of how time and time again, even after twenty-four years and the status of full professor, I find (as have many women in numerous professional settings), that a comment is ignored or not acknowledged only to have a male repeat the same points and have them highly praised. I and most of my female colleagues, even those who are physicians, consistently find that we are promoted less frequently, suffer significant salary inequities, and endure sexual harassment masked as compliments more often than not.

Yet my own stories and memories pale in the light of stories of my sisters in my own school and elsewhere. Physician Vanessa Northington Gamble recalls a patient asking a white male intern why "that girl" (Gamble) didn't clean-up when she was in his room, even though she had entered the room and spoken with the patient in her capacity as physician; both racism and sexism were at work here. Dr. September Williams, working late in the hospital of a predominantly white institution, reports asking the desk clerk to call a taxi for her and being ignored for an hour until she realized that if she did not identify herself specifically as a physician she would never get a cab. When she did so, the desk clerk asked, "Well, why didn't you say so earlier?"

One colleague tells of losing an internship because she called to check on her children and the babysitter during an informal conference at the very end of the working day. She was told such a call was inappropriate and indicative of her lack of commitment to the tasks. I think of how several women physicians were recently required to take a significant cut in pay and lost benefits in a restructuring plan; the male physicians in comparable positions were not so affected. (A chief administrative officer was heard to comment that "Women don't need as much money as men".) When a child of one of the female physicians overheard her commenting that the pay cut reduced her to a salary comparable to that of the nurses, the child queried, "Mommy, are you gonna be a nurse now?" So much for gender equity and role typing. Or I think of one colleague commenting on the "incredible challenge" associated with attempting to succeed in the medical academy, noting a constant awareness of the number of men who give women neither a fair shake nor respect. In her case in particular her efforts to be promoted have been repeatedly thwarted by her male colleagues despite the documented evidence of her meeting all the criteria. Women, she believes, are held to a higher standard. At the same time, she is aware of some female colleagues who are extremely negative. This she finds painful and baffling, leading to her confession that there are times when she feels more camaraderie with men.

Whether functioning in a predominantly black or white environment, African American females are frequently reminded of their invisibility and vulnerability, keeping them wondering when something unfairly negative happens if it is due to her gender or race or both. We find ourselves wondering, "Would this have happened if I were a man? Would this have happened if I were white?" There is a constant and painful self scrutiny that keeps us wondering just how much we are personally responsible for and accountable for our injuries, which is inseparable from the entire experience of being black in America. The coping strategies we use as women in a male dominated world often are exactly the strategies that we had to develop in order to negotiate our blackness in a white world. We learn not to "make waves," to make people like us, to place the burden of proof upon ourselves, to work actively at balancing and monitoring our responses, to be better than good. But at least in a predominantly black environment we are free of the double burden of assessing ourselves as both female and black. When we are able to determine when our femaleness is the issue, knowing is in some way a relief. Some of us fight back directly and vigorously. Others interpret the reality of our being "sheep in a cow's pasture" when we are in the male dominated world of medical school or hospital as requiring strategies of compromise and cunning that often appear to be capitulations.

For example, even now, after twenty-four years of being at my medical school, I rarely present myself before the faculty alone. I have learned to maximize a team approach, always involving a male physician as partner. I try hard to appear noncompetitive and generally defer to the power grabs of the men with whom I work. Although I can hear the feminist screams and protests, I can tell you that for me the strategy has worked. I have been able to develop the kind of curriculum I wanted, to conduct the kind of research I wished, and to move up within the administrative hierarchy, albeit more gradually than have the men. I now direct a program in clinical ethics, have a budget of my own, coordinate the activities of over thirty faculty, interface with the five schools and colleges of the Health Sciences Center, and have contact with over five hundred students.

Although tenured, my salary is still at least $10,000 below that of the men with comparable rank and responsibility. On the other hand, despite the conservative nature of the men with whom I work, there has been an opportunity to grow and be productive. Most of the women with whom I work have been quietly supportive and have been mentors and role models. Many of the men have as well. Despite role strain, occasional bouts of powerlessness and loneliness from time to time, the medical academy has afforded me an opportunity to have flexible hours, to function independently, to bring medical humanities and ethics into the curriculum as well as to juggle roles of wife, mother, and professional. Periodically I am still reminded that I am a woman in a medical environment in which women are not highly valued, despite the fact that our medical school graduated women much earlier than most and that today our classes are composed of at least fifty percent women.

The reality is that I am a humanist and a bioethicist in a setting where such persons are still extremely rare; thus my development within this system can and should be assessed as extremely positive in spite of the difficulties women face in that setting. Because of those continuing difficulties I see a need for constant vigilance and support systems to maintain and rebuild the ragged and tattered self-esteem of many women. I also see a need to confront, oh so gently, the male persons who have not a clue as to what they contribute to the problem, to educate them, to sensitize them, to develop sanctions for those who cannot and will not change—again, not so different from what we try to do in black/white relations. Admittedly, there is the very troubling reality that those women who seem to get along, do so by virtue of significant reconciliation with the unacceptable and by compromise. The capacity to understand, forgive, and rationalize appears to be an essential quality for most "successful" women in the medical academy along with the virtues of loyalty and commitment to a higher good. Unfortunately, in many instances those virtues also seem to contribute to our failure to protect ourselves, especially financially.

Finally, there is the need to appreciate that sheep have many wonderful positive qualities and may indeed at certain times and in certain places be far superior to cows, even if the cows don't know it. The problems are alive and enduring, but our capacity as women to adapt, to survive, and to persist is infinite.

PART III

Personal and Professional Identities

CHAPTER 13

The Echo of My Mother's Footsteps

◻

Rebekah Wang-Cheng

It is only recently that I have realized how much my mother has affected who I am and where I am in academic medicine today. As my older sisters and I have grown older we have remarked how we see our mother in our own mannerisms, traits and ways of doing things (Friday 1977). Although I had easily seen parallels in my personal life, I hadn't thought of my mother's impact on my career until I began writing this essay.

My mother is a feminist who probably doesn't even know the meaning of the word. The label is both ironic and appropriate for her at the same time: ironic because she was born in China, a patriarchal society and appropriate because she was born in 1912, which was a key turning point in China's long history. In 1912, the country was liberated after centuries of Manchurian domination and the republic of China was founded. That was the year "the last emperor" had to leave Peking and flee to Manchuria. Many people who saw the epic movie probably had no idea that the emperor was not really Chinese but a Manchurian foreigner. It was the year that my paternal grandmother cut off my grandfather's queue which had been forced on Chinese men as a symbol of loyalty to the Manchurian government.

The details of my mother's early life are sketchy because she hasn't told me much about them, either because she cannot remember or chooses not to. I don't know what happened to her parents, but she was raised by a kindly grandfather, and at a fairly young age was sent off to a boarding school. Recognizing her innate intelligence and talent, the Norwegian missionaries had selected her to go to England to study medicine, but instead she chose to marry my father, her major concession to the time she lived in. Nonetheless, in an era when many women still had bound feet and could not read, it is remarkable that she pursued her education through junior college and nurse's training.

Unfortunately, while I was growing up in the only Chinese family in a small Illinois town, I didn't understand what a pioneer my mother was. Instead

127

I was ashamed that my mother had a Chinese accent, not realizing what an accomplishment it was for her to come to the United States in her mid-thirties and pass the RN boards barely knowing the language.

Admiration for my mother's ability to successfully pursue a career in a new language and within an unfamiliar culture has propelled me to take an interest in the area of cross-cultural medicine. It is rarely a part of the formal curriculum of medical education in this country. A survey of the 126 U.S. medical schools found that only 13 included any training in this area (Lum and Korenman 1994). Without education and self-awareness, it is all too easy for physicians to impose our own stereotypes, health beliefs, and cultural norms on patients, especially when language barriers exist as well, resulting in a superficial approach to patient care. Of course this not only happens with people of a different ethnic background but also with patients who are different from us at all, be it by gender, political or religious persuasion, or socioeconomic background. Feminists in medical education need to lead the way in demonstrating respect for others as well as for ourselves, which leads me back to my mother's story.

She possessed tremendous amounts of self-respect, courage and faith enough to purchase a large old building that used to be part of a convent and begin a nursing home, even though she and my father had little money and four children to raise. It had long been a dream of theirs to establish either an orphanage or a nursing home.

Those early years were a struggle. When purchasing supplies from vendors over the phone, she would often be told, "Mrs. Wang, I really can't understand your English, why don't you just put this in writing to me?" She would feistily reply, "Well, you just stay on the line until I make you understand, or I call someone else." So it was from my mother that I learned that you could have your own voice, and if you persisted could even accomplish things. Believe me, the white mid-Western businessmen who were willing to deal with my diminutive Chinese mom ended up benefitting personally and financially.

Out of necessity she was forced to find her own voice; I understood that, but I was born and raised in America with all sorts of opportunities she didn't have. I had naively assumed that I would have no trouble being heard in academic medicine; that my needs, expectations, and aspirations would be listened to and taken seriously. Of course after several years I learned that I too needed to find my own voice and to speak clearly, usually in my own language, sometimes in a second language, but always retaining my own accent (Gilligan 1982). Just like my mother, often I would have to repeat myself, reiterate and translate until I was sure that the other person understood. Only then could a productive relationship result. After a decade of practice, I am no longer afraid when I am the only woman on a committee to speak up.

Even after forty years in America my mother still has a Chinese accent, but I love the sound of her voice. My embarrassment over my mother's broken

English was trivial compared to my shame that she was a working woman, and not just an ordinary working woman at that. She was the administrator and owner of a 49-bed nursing home. My family was already different, with a father who had a Ph.D. in clinical psychology. The rest of my friends had fathers who were either farmers, factory workers or salesmen. Regardless of how different his profession might have been, it was still okay for men to work, but women did not. This was the early sixties when there were fictional characters on television like June Cleaver, Donna Reed and Harriet Nelson, all of whom stayed at home cooking and cleaning and raising charming children.

My mother actually paid someone to come clean our house, and it still looked messy much of the time. I was continually afraid that my friends would find out that my mother didn't clean the house. In my eyes that somehow made her less of a woman.

In spite of my reservations about how she stacked up as a "normal woman," even in those early childhood years there was no doubt in my mind or heart that she was a great mother. No matter how tired she was from taking care of patients, doing tedious paperwork, and dealing with personnel problems, she took time to read to me, cook special dishes for me, and prod me to practice the piano or do homework. The amount of time I spent with her was also abundant even while she was working. When I wasn't playing at a friend's house, I spent my time at the nursing home talking to the patients, following my favorite nurses around, helping set trays in the kitchen and watching my mother deal with multiple responsibilities and difficulties with patience and humor. This is where my mother had the greatest influence on me, by living so well the combination of career and motherhood that I am now attempting to emulate.

When I began medical school in 1975, having a family was the furthest thing from my mind. For one thing, in my mind women either had careers or families, but did not do both at the same time seriously. My two older sisters had set a precedent by obtaining masters' degrees, working successfully in their fields, and then quitting when they had children. Although currently there are usually women faculty who combine family and career, during my medical school and residency training, most of the clinical women faculty that I encountered were either single, childless or had grown children.

Back in the late seventies, women medical students comprised about 10-20% of the classes. My medical school, Loma Linda University School of Medicine in southern California, did have a Women in Medicine (WIM) organization which was quite active. I don't recall whether or not we had a formal link with the American Medical Women's Association at the time. WIM's major function was to socialize and acculturate each successive younger class of women entering medicine.

On occasion we were agents of change, such as when a protest was made about slides of Playboy centerfolds that were snuck into the middle of lectures by male students presumably. Coming from a rather sheltered, conservative, Christian background, I was very impressed by the courage and unshaven legs of some of the student leaders of WIM. As part of a tongue-in-cheek response to WIM, the men in our class started an organization called BIM for "Bachelors in Medicine." Making t-shirts with their logo was probably their only accomplishment. One of those BIMs became my husband a few months prior to graduation.

It amazes me now, when I think back to that time, that I could actually graduate from medical school without a clear vision for my future career. I attribute that mainly to a lack of role models and mentors. Psychiatry seemed to be a natural choice for me, since I had majored in behavioral sciences in college and was somewhat acquainted with the field because of my father. However, I did not receive any formal guidance and only once do I recall being given advice by a teacher. On a pediatric surgery rotation, a surgeon remarked to me, "you're too active to go into psychiatry; you should consider internal medicine or pediatrics." Those words came back to haunt me during my internship in psychiatry. There did seem to be a lot of sitting around in psychiatry, and I really did enjoy the faster pace on my medicine rotations. In the winter of my internship, I made arrangements to switch to internal medicine at the end of the academic year. It was a difficult but crucial decision for me, and I am still grateful to the busy surgeon who took the time to share his observations with me.

At the Medical College of Wisconsin, each junior student has a formal career advisor who helps plan the senior year. Some faculty are not willing to take on yet another responsibility, but because of my own experience (which I've shared numerous times with students), I make a special point to serve as advisor for four or five students each year. Informally, I also query students with whom I work in the hospital or clinics about their specialty choices. Women students in particular tend to seek me out or ask questions about internal medicine, academic versus private practice, and how I combine career and family in my field.

I do not regret my psychiatric training; in fact it has continued to be a major interest of mine. In addition to having a secondary appointment in the Department of Psychiatry, I remain active in the field as behavioral medicine coordinator for our primary care internal medicine track, and director of a psychological medicine clinic. I emphasize to students that education is never wasted, and that we always have choices.

Not too long after I made the momentous decision to change from psychiatry to internal medicine, I was on attending rounds in nephrology one morning when I developed an abrupt stomach queasiness. After a few mornings of this, and a careful check of the calendar, I realized that the unthinkable must be true. Now that I had a clear focus for my career, the last thing I wanted was to have a major interruption . . . like a child. My husband, who was also a medicine resident, and I received a lot of good-natured teasing about how two physicians could end up with such a preventable mistake. Of course the initial teasing was nothing compared to what we received after I found myself pregnant for the second time, only nine months after our first son was born. At my graduation banquet, it was no surprise when I received the "fertile female physician award."

Fortunately, for both of these children, the residency program director was most accommodating. He permitted me to take a four-month leave of absence with each birth and to arrange my schedule, so that when my husband was on a tough rotation with lots of night call, I could be on an elective and vice-versa. That made it much easier on our child caregivers, and also enabled me be able to breast-feed both of the children until they were about one year old. When I was on overnight call in the hospital, my husband would bring Christopher into the sleeping room so I could nurse him; fortunately, we only lived about five minutes away from the hospital.

By the time my second son Andrew was six-months old, I had finished my residency, but my husband had decided to take another residency in anesthesiology. He was staying at Loma Linda, so I was pleased to be offered a faculty position in general medicine since I had enjoyed the informal teaching of medical students and interns while a resident. I didn't really view the position as the first step in an academic medicine career, but simply as a convenient job since my husband needed to remain in the area.

Thus, my entry into academic medicine was just as unplanned as my children. And like my children, my career has been rewarding, frustrating and challenging. I also discovered how important both were to me: while I was on maternity leave, I missed the stimulation of medicine, but after long days in the hospital, I also missed the simple pleasures of being with my children. Working part-time seemed to be the best solution, for then I had sufficient energy to do justice to both.

In 1985, after two years of teaching, I was certain that academic medicine was for me. That year my husband finished his fellowship and was recruited by the Medical College of Wisconsin. I negotiated for a part-time position at the same institution, and soon found out that I would be a second-class citizen because of it. My title would be different—I would be a "clinical assistant professor," which was the same designation given to volunteer unpaid faculty. I also would not receive any health insurance, disability, retirement, malpractice coverage, life insurance or sick days, even on a pro-rated basis. Since I was committed to spending some time with my young sons, I accepted all of this without question, and was just grateful to have a part-time academic position.

Two years after I joined the division of general medicine, a new division chief arrived who was a charismatic, energetic leader. He had two daughters and was married to a pediatrician who worked part-time, and so was very understanding and supportive of the needs of professional women. Our division grew to about twenty faculty, half of whom were women. Of these women, about two-thirds had part-time arrangements like myself. Our chief not only suggested but also provided financial support for the women to have a half-day retreat to discuss some of the issues for women in academic medicine. Later from that small beginning, a department-wide retreat was held for women. Many issues were discussed, such as mentorship, networking, combining career and family, advancement in rank, and leadership. We submitted a report to the Dean of the medical school, and he responded by forming a Women's Faculty Council, and appointed me to be one of its members.

Shortly after my new chief arrived, he instituted weekly faculty meetings. Since he came to the office at 5:00 a.m., he thought that a 7:00 a.m. meeting time would be quite reasonable. Although our male colleagues were probably not enamored by this early morning meeting, none of them spoke out publicly against it. We women however got together and wrote a formal letter of protest to him, explaining the hardship it placed on us, our families and our child-caregivers. His creative response was to develop an administrative half-day for the division, where in addition to the 9:00 a.m. business meeting, faculty members would have more time for meeting together on projects or doing their own individual research. This resulted in enhanced faculty morale and productivity. How? That first effort of a few women led to a group effort to look at other issues that affect women, eventually resulting in a major change at the medical school level for part-time faculty.

The following year, 1988, was a highly significant year for me personally. Just when my career was starting to become focused, and the children were in school, I found myself pregnant again. This pregnancy was more emotionally, rather than physically traumatic for me, especially when I learned that it would be another boy. It took some time for me to come to terms with having another child in my mid-thirties. Eventually, through the resilience and perseverance inherited and/or learned from my mother, I worked hard to finish a medical education research project. While eight months pregnant, I presented the results at the National Society of General Internal Medicine meeting, just before taking yet another leave of absence from my career.

Several months later, in that same year, I received notification that I had been elected by the senior class to the Alpha Omega Alpha Honor Society. This recognition by the students meant so much, because for me, the personal joy and fulfillment from academic medicine comes from teaching and interacting with students and residents. It was particularly meaningful, coming at a time when I felt that once again my career would be idling for a while.

In 1989, the school finally developed a formal track for part-time faculty designated as the "full professional effort" track. By definition, all academically qualified faculty who devote full professional effort to programs of the college, working at least half-time (which is considered 1,000 hours per year), but not working full-time, are eligible for appointment to this faculty category. These faculty have the responsibilities of full-time faculty and are eligible for the same faculty rank and title as would be appropriate for full-time faculty. The same appointment and promotion procedures are applied, except that full professional effort faculty cannot be considered for tenure.

In 1991, I became the first person to be promoted on that track when I became Associate Professor. This formal recognition of my professional competence was very gratifying to me. I had worked hard to gain credibility as a serious clinician educator. Even though I was not physically visible at work as much as full-time faculty, I developed research projects and accepted administrative responsibilities, appointments to committees, an equal share of ward attending months and after-hour calls. Of course much of the work I did was on my "own time," but being part-time actually gave me more autonomy and control over my time. I could choose whether to spend my afternoon going to the library story hour with my son or writing a manuscript.

My colleagues have accepted and respect my dual roles. At first I was apologetic and sometimes worried that my commitments to my children would be negatively perceived, but over the years I have gained courage. Recently, when I matter-of-factly cancelled a meeting because I was taking the morning off to go on a field trip to the zoo with the kindergarten class, my male colleagues not only did not blink, but were supportive of me. My patients also understand that I am not available to see them every single day. I think they appreciate that I am a better physician because I am a mother, and I know because of my experiences as a physician that I am a better mother.

If I could think of one concept or key word that has characterized my life's career, it would be collaboration. I think that one of the greatest strengths that women possess is the ability to work with other people, to share power and information without feeling personally diminished or threatened.

One woman can probably make a difference, but I do not believe she needs to attempt it alone; my own experience has shown many times over that there are other women and men who will cooperate and work together to make a difference. And there are other women from other generations who have forged their own unique paths in their own way. If we listen clearly, we can hear the echo of their footsteps, just as I hear my mother's.

CHAPTER 14

How Medicine Tried to Make a Man Out of Me
(And Failed, Finally)

❑

Lucy M. Candib

There seems to have been a race between our becoming, for example, professors [or doctors], and our sufficiently changing the world for it to be morally acceptable for us to occupy such positions. This was not, of course, a race we could win; we were, that is, doomed to succeed (those of us who did succeed, and, of course, not all did) more quickly than we could change the world. We told ourselves, in part, that we were succeeding precisely in order to have the power to change the world, but the result is that we have become, structurally, "them." The moral questions we now face turn not on purity (hopelessly unavailable to us) but on acceptable, politically accountable, compromise: can we live the positions we occupy differently enough?

—Scheman (1993, ix)

Twenty years ago when I was younger (I am now 48), single (I am now in a committed relationship), living with a woman (my partner now is a man) and without children (I now have 2 children, almost 6 and 11), I joined a brand-new family practice residency program as a second year resident. It had been my dream for years to practice in a neighborhood health center, and here was my perfect chance: a training program in an urban health center set in a working-class community. Let me say at the outset that the health center was not then, nor is it now, a feminist organization. It was not a feminist women's health collective, nor a women's health center, nor an outgrowth of the women's movement. It was, and is, a community based center, with consumer, fiscal, and business interests strongly represented on its board of directors.

Frances Anthes, John Myers, Richard Schmitt, Randy Wertheimer, and Rachel Wheeler all provided thoughtful commentary on previous drafts of this chapter.

When I came to Worcester, two recently trained male family physicians, hired the year before the residency opened, served both as the medical staff of the health center as well as the faculty for the training program. ("Faculty" held university appointments but were employees of the health center.) One of the two original faculty members, John Frey, became my friend, mentor, and sponsor. Two other men, an executive director and a business manager, ran the organization administratively, fiscally, and ideologically. Though almost all the nursing, social work, and clerical staff were women, the health center was clearly run by men. And because I was delighted to be where I wanted to be, doing what I wanted to do, mostly with other women and on behalf of women, I was oblivious initially to the patriarchal (i.e., male dominated) nature of the institution.

After two years, I finished the training program and joined the two male physicians as a faculty member. Committed to women's health, I became the first faculty member to do obstetrics, and remained the only faculty member taking call for obstetrics for several years. Anyone with a glimmer of knowledge of medical systems will know that this was an enormous and exhausting commitment. I understand now what was unspoken then, that I was being shaped by the forces of stress universally experienced by women physicians in that period: prejudice, lack of role models, and role strain (Bowman and Allen 1985). It was during those years (although certainly not the first time) that medicine did its best to make a man out of me.

Highly visible to residents as a role model, I was seeing patients eight or nine sessions a week and doing obstetrics. When one intern found herself pregnant in the fall of her internship, it was natural that she turn to me to be her doctor. And with this dual relationship of doctor/teacher came some of the most conflictual professional feelings I have ever sustained. What she must have hoped for from me, her teacher and her doctor, I can only imagine: support, encouragement, patience, permission to modify her training, respect for her choices, acceptance. What I hoped for from her, the first resident to get pregnant in our training program, was a model pregnant physician who would magically manage the demands of pregnancy and internship without missing a beat. Projecting my own unrealistic standards onto her, I wanted nothing more than the model pregnancy, natural childbirth, and perfect motherhood, combining breast feeding with full-time return to residency.

Don't laugh; remember, this was the late 1970s.

Needless to say, given our expectations, we disappointed each other in terribly painful ways, more painful for her because, I understand now, she was far more vulnerable to me than I was to her. Today, after dozens of pregnant residents have trained in our system, I see all too well how conflictual were the roles of doctor and teacher and how I failed her in my inability to manage the power difference between doctor-teacher and trainee-patient. But rather than dwell on my personal failings, I want to examine how the overall male-dominated power alignments dictated the outcome. Isolated as the only woman faculty member, I felt that each woman trainee was a standard-bearer for our cause. Essentially a token in male medicine, we had to be better than good. In the male corporate structure of the 1970s, token status meant that all eyes were on our performance. The ways that I was critical of her were, of course, my responsibility, but I, too, had been shaped to judge myself in terms of how I bent my energies to serve the masculine priorities of medicine and the health center. Unbeknownst to me, and certainly to her, at that point in my career I was exhibiting the shortage of empathy and responsiveness to others and conforming to the dominant achievement standards of the times in a way now understood to be typical of women doctors from my age cohort (Cartwright and Wink 1994). Looking back, I now locate my worst remorse in having become an instrument of the patriarchy in my dealings with this young woman doctor at a point of crisis in her life and her medical education.

How will she respond to this draft? Is this essay just another attempt to heal this mess from years ago?

After another few years, the various male faculty members moved on to greener pastures. We had hired one male faculty member fresh out of training. After a year he demanded and got a raise to a salary higher than mine, despite my seniority. I blew several gaskets. ("Come on, it's only a few dollars more," they told me.) I insisted on a comparable raise, and he left after another year. A search for a new, presumably male, medical director was unsuccessful. Finally the administration, still composed of the same two administrators and now a woman grantswriter (formerly the secretary to the executive director), reluctantly accepted the fact that I would have to become medical director. (In that era, men felt that men make better supervisors, that women were temperamentally unfit.)

I took on the job of "acting" medical director in 1980, when there were few family physicians completing training, and far fewer who wanted to work in the depressed inner city, do obstetrics, and teach, all at a laughably low salary. At that point I was the only faculty member. I immediately hired the three graduating residents to serve as faculty and spent the next few years feeling like a single mother with several teenagers and a dozen younger children, struggling to make ends meet and keep everyone fed and clothed. Among Kanter's (1977) now-familiar stereotyped roles available to me as a token woman leader, I was perpetually caught between mother and iron maiden.

Those were tough times. One resident told the residency director that I "never blinked." I had one half-day of administrative time; today the medical director does administration six half-days each week.

As the medical director, I was at the intersection between the demands of the administration on the faculty and residents, and the demands of the faculty and residents back to the administration. Administration played by the numbers; patient visits were the bottom line. Faculty wanted better salaries and benefits and time for research, administration, and education. Residents wanted fewer service commitments and more focus on education. I was caught between the appearance of power I held over the staff and trainees and the reality of powerlessness I occupied in the halls of the administration. While I know now that the power of middle-management positions is always ambiguous, I have since learned that the powerlessness I felt was characteristic of token women in the corporate structures of that era.

Being a woman at this intersection of conflicting interests meant that the staff expected me to be giving, supportive, and sustaining; the administration was threatened by me, didn't trust me, and used a variety of techniques to keep me isolated, uninformed, and disempowered. For example, the executive director consistently badmouthed the psychologist who ran our companion mental health center, thus guaranteeing that we would never talk to each other. When the psychologist and I finally sat down together years later, we learned how we had been supplied with enough negative commentary about the other to fill a tractor trailer and to ensure our mutual isolation. In addition, the executive director consistently maintained a sexist atmosphere by telling dirty jokes and humiliating women staff. In this extreme climate of stress, it is hard to believe I stayed in the job. I now understand what held me and other women physicians like me was the deep commitment to patients and to work in the community.

The head of the social work department had arranged for the whole agency to undergo a training on child sexual abuse. For two half-days the health center operated on skeleton crews while we attended the meetings. At the end, like dozens of other women no doubt before me, I approached the trainers, and asked, "Does this mean that what my father's cousin did to me was sexual abuse?" As I grappled with this reinterpretation of my childhood over the next few months, I also started to look at my job differently. On the day of the annual picnic, I sat down across from a new male intern. The executive director sat down next to him and began his usual banter with "My problem is, I want to go out with my secretary's daughter [age 10] but she won't let me." I responded instantly, emphatically, "That is totally inappropriate." He never forgave me for humiliating him in front of another man. I began to realize that, for those already sensitized, sexual harassment in the workplace recapitulates childhood sexual abuse.

Within this crisscrossing constellation of conflicts, I want to talk about how the system I have described tried to mandate my betrayal of women faculty. The young women physicians whom I recruited and hired to be faculty began getting pregnant. Like women physicians elsewhere, the women faculty at the health center had postponed pregnancy till late in training or the first years after completion of training. Married, more often than not, to male physicians, they anticipated cutting back their hours and working part-time. One of the faculty, Rachel Wheeler, and her husband both chose to work part-time from the very beginning, anticipating their family. As luck would have it, three of us had four babies in eighteen months. Meredith Martin, who had been full-time, went to part-time with her second child, and Rachel remained part-time but felt increasingly put upon by the administration's lack of recognition of her commitment. At 37, I too got pregnant and delivered and went half-time for six months after my maternity leave. Thus, there were three of us who nursed, pumped, took full night call, and delivered our own patients whenever we had child care.

Rachel learned to ask all her depressed patients about sexual abuse. It was overwhelming when they all answered yes.

The administration saw our pregnancies as shortchanging the health center and publically insinuated that because we were part-time we were less committed. ("The problem with the health center is that there are too many part-timers.") The administration questioned Rachel's right to a maternity leave for an adopted baby and provoked lasting outrage. Yet despite my inherently feisty nature, I found myself immobilized and unable to fight back. As the medical director I was responsible to make sure the work got done, and it did get done, but at great cost. As each of us went on maternity leave, the others shouldered more call. Maternity leave, though an explicit employee benefit, became the scapegoat for the problems facing the health center—including the shortage of family doctors willing to work in the inner city at low pay. Beyond the health center, medicine was still not ready to acknowledge the legitimacy of maternity leave for women physicians. Stories abound of heroic women who returned to work after two weeks so as not to burden their colleagues with extra call.

I too felt burdened by the tyranny of the short-staffing and frequent call, and found myself unwittingly buying into the administration's worldview that part-time was less committed. As I look back on that time, I think this temporary default was due to the pressures of pitting home against partners. After a year of this, I knew that I wanted to stop being medical director of an unworkable system and go part-time myself. At that point the administration threatened to withdraw payment of our malpractice insurance (an employee benefit equal to approximately a third of the physician's part-time salary) at a time when malpractice insurance costs were rising exponentially. This threat generated an all-out war between the faculty doctors and the executive director that was ultimately resolved only by appeal to the Board of Directors.

My stomach gets knotted up just thinking of that meeting. The executive director was punitive and hostile. I felt angry and betrayed. I knew I might lose the staff over this one. The Board liked to think that it was just a "personality conflict" between him and me. They had no conception of how toxic he was for a sexual abuse survivor. If sexual harassment had been a legitimate claim in those days, there is no question of how I might have proceeded. It is also clear to me that the job, as it was structured, was a typical "survivor" job— overworked, mercilessly critical of myself and too often others, trapped between feeling victimized and angry, I traced all too familiar a pattern.

It took this kind of threat—which, if realized, would have caused us all to resign—to enable me to join my women colleagues in the fight for reasonably paid part-time employment for committed women physicians during our child-bearing years. Individually, we were vulnerable; united, we had a chance to succeed at our collective goal (Lorber 1984).

In the uneasy truce that followed, I spent the next year recruiting a new (male) medical director, and finally managed to arrange my life in a more balanced fashion. (Later Canadian research confirms that women physicians who spend an average of 37 hours per week on professional activities "seldom" feel overwhelmed, while those feeling overwhelmed or overloaded more than once a week devote, on average, 43 hours a week to work [Brown 1992]. It truly is a fine line.) But I now know that for a time I was unsupportive to those very women who had the same deep commitments to patient care and to family life as I had. And I now believe the male dominated forces that had shaped my family of origin and organized my work life put me in the position of defending exactly the kind of medical practice that was hostile to women. I see because I, too, by this time shared the commitment to a child and a relationship, I was able to join the struggle on behalf of women. The three of us who had had the four babies wrote and published an article on women physicians working part-time (Wheeler, Martin, and Candib 1988), and looking back now, perhaps it did all work out for the best.

I'm not saying you have to get pregnant and have a baby to see the light; I'm saying that's what it took for me to "get it."

Rocky times followed. We felt that we were seeing patients as fast as we could, but the administration threatened that unless we saw more, none of the employees would get a raise. Amidst charts of productivity quotas and threats of salary freezes, the executive director fired the subsequent medical director without due process. The only other male physician had already turned in his resignation, and the four women physicians had no recourse except to resign. We wrote a group letter of resignation. *If he could fire the medical director just like that, what kind of place were we working for?* Rachel remembers hoping that someone would figure out that something must be wrong for all the doctors to resign, but nothing happened.

Thus, all the physicians all made plans to leave, prompting two doctors to come over from the medical school to try to bail the center out. Six months later, with the practice in a shambles around me, I had no heart to look for another job. Survivor mentality? I don't know, but I withdrew my resignation hoping against the odds that I could outlast the executive director who seemed hellbent on driving the center into the ground. Fortunately for me and the center, he made a fatal solipsistic error—he submitted his resignation, apparently thinking that the Board would rally around him and refuse to accept it. Instead, the chairperson accepted his resignation, announced to the newspaper that his tenure of seventeen years was over, and he was out of a job.

Some good work came out of those years. Together with a psychology graduate student I brought together a group of women physicians who wrote and published a paper about how our pregnancies changed our relationships with patients (Candib et al. 1987). Rachel and I became closer friends with our children so close in age. Even though she left the health center during the mass resignation, she brought her family medicine commitment to another neighborhood health center, and once a month she still comes back to teach our residents. She is now the president of the Massachusetts Academy of Family Physicians, and I take enormous pleasure in having been her preceptor, supervisor, mentor, and friend.

Rachel tells me her fierce anger erupts these days with the husbands of her female partners who still expect the woman to do all the transport and arrange all the childcare.

My experience as a woman of those years is only one part of a complex story. I have not talked about the deep feelings of inferiority or class difference that may have provoked the director's need to constantly diminish me and any other person who had the potential to challenge him. I have not talked about the racism that African-American or Puerto Rican employees might have experienced from the same man nor the more overt sexual harassment. I have not talked about the residents who felt educationally abused by me and by a system that took their work for granted. I have not talked about the men who may have longed for a paternity leave or the ability to work part-time so that they could spend more time with their families. I have only suggested the outline of the experience of women physicians who were privileged yet oppressed in the workings of one medical institution.

It is years later and the health center is very different. The male administrators are gone, and the current executive director is the very same woman who started out as secretary to the executive director almost twenty-five years ago. More than half of the ten physicians are women, and half of us are part-time. Seven of the eight nurse practitioners are women and half of them are part-time as well. Last year twelve out of thirteen residents were women. Frequently, afternoon chart rounds consists of a social worker, psychologist or psychiatrist, a faculty member, and five or six residents and an occasional medical student. Not uncommonly, all of us are women. In the last two years four women residents and three women faculty have had eight babies. At chart rounds this week I found myself encouraging a soon-to-be third year resident to consider part-time status. *This, I told her, is already your life. Your baby will not be this age again. You could spend more time with her now and you will find yourself less resentful toward the work. Residency is supposed to teach practice management, and that means practicing now how you hope to practice later, rather than putting it all on hold and hating it in the process.*

Elsewhere the traditional organization and ethos of medicine still expects a full-time professional with full-time backup at home. Medicine is still a "greedy" profession, eating up the life of the one at work and the one at home as well. Men like Rachel's husband, John Myers, who have chosen to work part-time, find themselves coerced into full-time work when staffing is tight because administrators do not take seriously their commitment to personal and family life. And the standards of achievement set up during medical training continue to make it hard for men to believe that part-time work represents a "success." As a result, most men do not expect to modify their medical careers for family life, and most women do. Medicine, and society in general, accepts this arrangement happily since it does not challenge the gendered power relations either at home or at work.

Challenges to the gendered division of labor will need to happen both in medical institutions and in the relationships of medical men and women. Medicine will gobble up just as much of people's lives as they let it; at the individual level, how men and women work out their relationships will determine just how much and whom medicine gets to devour. For the moment, at our center, the medical staff is now large enough to tolerate several maternity leaves a year. In this setting, the flexibility that the women have adapted in planning their work lives now enables the men physicians to consider part-time work as children enter their lives as well. It would appear that we have made some progress.

But then perhaps not. Recently John Frey, still a good friend and now a well-known family medicine educator, received a standing ovation after a keynote address. In his talk, he told stories about patients he had taken care of over the years and stories of the doctors he had interviewed who had stayed in their communities for over thirty years. I have known John for twenty years: as a teacher, as a clinician, as a man who has suffered in private and public ways. I am well acquainted with the historical and artistic and clinical sources on which he draws to portray his stories of family doctors. We have shared books, images, mentors, and mutual love of the work of family medicine. And yet something in his speech disturbed me. Even though I have now practiced family medicine in one community for those twenty years and even though I have stayed on like those doctors whose stories he tells, I could not find myself in his talk.

Afterwards I tell John that there are no women in his world of family medicine. "But, Luce, that's just the way they write." "No, John, they are only writing about men."

When John quotes John Berger, in *A Fortunate Man*, that the task of the doctor is "to recognize the man," I begin to see how deeply buried is the masculinist ethic within family medicine:

> This can be achieved by the doctor presenting himself to the patient as a comparable man. It demands from the doctor a true imaginative effort and precise self-knowledge. The patient must be given the chance to recognize, despite his aggravated self-consciousness, aspects of himself in the doctor, but in such a way that the doctor seems to be Everyman. (1976, 76)

The icon of the community family physician is still a white man, one hundred per cent dedicated to practice, whose life is managed and supported by a full-time wife and mother whose image is missing from the admired portrait. Women physicians juggling part-time schedules, sharing practices with nurse practitioners, pumping milk on their lunch hours, and racing back from the office to the day care center, these women are still invisible in the idealized imagery of family medicine.

Let's not even mention gay and lesbian doctors and doctors of color. Talk about invisible.

How different it would be if we thought of the doctor presenting herself to the patient as a "comparable woman," if the patient could find aspects of herself in the doctor in such a way that the doctor seems to be Everywoman. This is a very different image of family medicine, and indeed, medicine in general, that we have yet to imagine. We are short on stories, images, and poetry to tell about this way of being Everywoman. As I rose to join the standing ovation after John's talk, I knew in the act of clapping that medicine is still trying to make a man of me, of all of us. Even as I do the work I love, I find myself and women like me and women of color not like me invisible and unrepresented in the medical world that is still my home. Despite the palpable reality of my hard-working presence, when my friend holds up his mirror, I still cannot see myself. When will this change?

But you are talking about DOCTORS. What about all those women washing patients, lifting bedpans, changing diapers, toting laundry? Who's going to hold up a mirror for them?

The health center is a small place in the larger scale of things, but when I look in its reflection I can see myself in the image of the women, and some men, joining together with nurse practitioners and social workers to practice community-based family medicine. Though it is still not an explicitly feminist institution, women are central in its leadership and direction. Though class and race issues are still divisive, they are more open for discussion than ever before. Much more work on behalf of women patients and their families has become possible in a setting where staff, practitioners, and administrators share with patients some kinds of common experiences as women. When this shared reality becomes the stuff of keynote addresses, then I'll be the first one up for the standing ovation. In the meantime, I hit twenty years this week, and it's just ten more until John comes to interview me. And I think by then I will be able to answer Naomi Scheman's question in the affirmative: Yes, I have been able to live the position I occupy differently enough.

CHAPTER 15

Moments of Becoming: After Virginia Woolf

□

Beth Alexander

January 1974

> First, are you our sort of person?
> Do you wear
> A glass eye, false teeth or a crutch,
> A brace or a hook,
> Rubber breasts or a rubber crotch,
> Stitches to show something's missing?
>
> —Sylvia Plath (1961, 4)

It wasn't a good interview. The questions from the committee, all men, still plague me.

"Just why is it you decided at age 28 to become a doctor?"

"Does your husband know about this?"

"We've never had a woman with children before as a medical student. We've had some 'accidents' with our female students, but they mostly had to drop out. Just what do you plan to do with your children?"

"What did you do for Planned Parenthood? Why did you work for them?"

"What do you believe about abortion?"

"Why are you not satisfied with your job as a counsellor?"

"Do you think women can stand the physical stress of this profession?"

"Do you plan to work full-time?"

A week later, I still find myself offended. What does being a mother have to do with it? They told me that I was the first woman with children ever to apply. Can this really be true? My grades and MCAT scores are good enough for Harvard. How can they fail to see that? Are my credentials invisible, masked by my status as a wife and mother? By the end of the interview, I found myself believing in the validity of their questions, and doubting my goals and my right to be there. They sounded just like my mother, who believes women should only be teachers or nurses, and then only as a "fall-back" job. Will I have to be a widow in order to enjoy a career? This is the seventies. I thought we had equal opportunity, as well as the vote. Perhaps not yet.

March 1974

> The old woman I shall become will be quite
> different from the woman I am now.
> Another I is beginning.
>
> —George Sand (1992, 189)

The mailman arrived with the letter today. "Congratulations! You are accepted into the entering class . . ." What sweet words. I ran down to catch up with the postal cart and threw my arms around him, gave the postman a hug, and told him the news. Startled, he asked me the *same* questions that the admissions committee asked. "But what will you do with your children, and your husband?" I am the first woman with children admitted to my medical school. It seems everyone is curious about what I will do with my family.

September 1974

> Just because everything is different
> doesn't mean anything has changed.
>
> —Irene Porter (1992, 28)

Medical school seems like a constant balance, determining when to stay silent and invisible, and when to challenge. I thought the days of being seen and not heard were over. Now I note that I am neither seen nor heard. All of my competencies, as a mother, as a counselling professional, flew out the window when I came here. I note that professors say things as if I'm not in the room. "Women with children belong at home," I heard today from the pathology professor. What does *that* have to do with pathology? I wonder how my children are this morning, negotiating kindergarten and second grade. I wonder if this choice, to pursue this career is harmful to them. They seem okay.

December 1975

> Silence was the haunted field
> each walked home through
> alone, afraid that to cry out
> was to give away her position.
>
> —Anita Skeen (unpublished)

I look around me in the classroom at my colleagues. I note the women are more silent in lecture than the men. For every three comments or questions offered by men, only one is asked by a woman. The silence of the women here is a mine field of unspoken stories, of invisible knowledge, of personal power not yet detonated. When we have lectures on heart disease, I note that the illustrations are only about men; when we have lectures on mental illness or hypochondriasis, only women are the patients. Most disturbing is the look of belief and acceptance on the faces of so many students around me. When professors describe patients, *what isn't said* is more noticeable than *what is said.* I start to notice whose stories are left out, who is not in the pictures in the textbook, in whose name the story is being told, and from whose perspective. Who benefits from this view of the world? Whose rules form the framework for the telling of these "truths?"

May 1977

It is never too late to be what you might have been.

—George Eliot (1992, 38)

It is over. It is just beginning, they say. I have graduated, first in my class of 200. This is not so much an honor as a statement about my determination never to have the admissions committee doubt that women with children can be competent medical students. I am going into family medicine, against much protest. The faculty have tried to persuade me that this is not a specialty worth my ability. "You're too smart to go into family practice." "Won't you be uncomfortable with having to keep current on such broad areas?" "Why waste your training taking care of colds and flu?" These are the most common questions that are raised. On the other hand, the faculty talk about needing physicians with a broad range of skills to practice in rural sites, to handle everything that comes up. Do they want only "poorer" students for this task? I thought there was honor in valuing relationships with patients, in taking care of the "whole person," the whole family. Why is it that the clinical faculty are not more concerned about what would make me happy rather than claiming my entry into their specialty as a victory over other specialties? Is this really about taking care of patients, or is it about power? Over other specialties, over students, over patients at times? I am happy with my career choice. I only wonder if I am strong enough to handle the frequent put downs about family medicine, if I can keep my vision of what I wish to do, in spite of the disapproval of other physicians. Most physicians are addicted to approval. Perhaps that has been part of my training, also.

February 1979

> Do not go gentle into that good night,
> Old age should burn and rave at close of day;
> Rage, rage against the dying of the light.
>
> —Dylan Thomas (1976, 339)

I am responsible for my first dying patient. Mildred, who is a closeted lesbian and has yet to tell me that the woman she has lived with for the past forty-five years is not really her cousin, has end stage sarcoma. I sit with her in the evening after finishing rounds, and she thanks me for all I've done for her. This is an offering that is hard to accept. Why do I feel like a failure? What is it I've been taught? I start to cry as she offers gratitude, and she hands me Kleenex. All of the proscriptions I've been taught in the past four years about what *not* to do in these situations comes galloping into my consciousness. "Don't get too close to your patients; you will lose your objectivity." "Don't cry in front of patients; it's unprofessional." "Don't complain about your hours; you made your bed . . ." "Don't share any personal information with patients; they will misconstrue it." Cut off a part of yourself; be invisible . . . Mildred and I talk about Judith and how frightened she is of being alone. I'm not sure what to say to her that is genuine, especially if I have to follow all the "rules" at the same time. The air is heavy with unspoken thoughts, mine as well as Mildred's. They tangle in the uncertainty of what we can say to each other. There have been no lectures on how to sit with dying patients.

October 1982

> I am the woman
> offering two flowers
> whose roots
> are twin.
> Justice and Hope.
> Let us begin.
>
> —Alice Walker (1984, 1)

SN told me today her husband has a gun. He has threatened to kill her. She is afraid, not so much for herself, but for her children. I delivered her last child, Kim, who is now a gorgeous two year old. Violence against women is normal in her culture, she has told me. I cannot ever understand why her husband would want to kill her, although from the intensity of her fear, I believe her. I offered to get her to the battered women's shelter, asked her if she had friends she could stay with. She said she needed to leave town, to become unnoticeable, so she couldn't be found. My nurse drove her to the bus station. Again I find myself thinking about boundaries. I wanted to give her money, but didn't know if she would be offended. I offered to call the police on her behalf, and she refused. What is my responsibility? Why would anyone want to kill such a meek, quiet woman? What could she have done? What can I do? She plans to return home after she goes to visit her sister in Oklahoma. The kids will be with her. She will be invisible for awhile now, and safe.

December 1982

There is nothing one man will not do to another.

–Carolyn Forché (1981,15)

SN was shot and killed. I suspect by her husband, although I don't know for sure. I called the police detective today, to report what she told me the last time I saw her. He said, "We don't get involved in these things. It would make things worse, rather than better, in the Vietnamese community. This kind of violence is normal for them." The words still ring in my ears. Better for whom? Normal, by whose standards? The detective's? My rage burns like the coals in front of me in this December fireplace. I feel helpless. They told me the father would probably keep the children. What will I do if he brings them in to see me at my office? I tried to talk with one of my partners today about it, but his response was not helpful. He implied that I was too emotionally involved. He said it was unlikely that there was anything I could do that would be helpful. SN was right. Her husband *was* going to kill her. If she had shot him, would the response would have been the same?

September 1984

Because I could not stop for Death
He kindly stopped for me.

–Emily Dickinson (1890, 712)

I saw Susan today, for the first time as a patient. She had asked me to talk with her about birth control and do her pap smear, as she hadn't has one in more than five years, and she was just past forty. She promised she'd be no trouble as a patient, because she was "healthy as a horse." I asked her how she'd gotten her birth control pills without an exam, and she told me one of the ob/gyn faculty just kept refilling the prescription; this was not what he had taught us in lecture. The minute I saw her breast, I knew she had cancer. I didn't even have to feel it, I could see it. I could easily find enlarged axillary nodes as well. She took the news calmly. As if I were telling her about finding a hemorrhoid. We talked about mastectomy, about radiation and chemotherapy, about getting lots of information before she made choices, about telling Fred. All of my blood seemed stuck in my toes when she left. She didn't seem as upset as I was. I'm already sure she will die of this disease. The cancer is too big. It has spread too far. How could she not know it was there? How could Fred not know? How could my colleague have prescribed birth control pills for nearly six years without an exam? How could this breast cancer be so invisible for so long?

September 1985

> The heart is the toughest part of the body,
> Tenderness is in the hands.
>
> —Carolyn Forché (1981, 23)

Susan has a recurrence. Her cancer has spread to her nodes, her liver, and bone. She asked me to take care of her. She trusts me. She wants to stay out of the hospital, to be with Fred, to keep active as long as possible. We talked about the dilemmas of my being both her friend and her doctor. It seems there are advantages and disadvantages to that. We agreed that I would use one of my colleagues as a litmus test for objectivity whenever I had doubts, to protect her and to protect me. I guess if I were dying of breast cancer, I would want someone to take care of me whom I considered a friend. My colleagues tell me I'm nuts to do this; that you can't mix friendship with care. Where did that rule come from? I'm not sure. When I think about the patients I am most close to, I find similarities between those relationships and the ones I have with my close friends. Trust. Honesty. Commitment. Caring. Perhaps not mutuality. Or vulnerability that is shared. I'm protected. My vulnerability in this case is going to be a bit hard to hide. I am losing a friend. I need to call National Cancer Institute and M.D. Anderson to make sure there are no other useful therapeutic alternatives.

December 1, 1985

> . . . and therefore never send to know for
> whom the bell tolls; it tolls for thee.
>
> —John Donne (1990, 344)

Susan died this morning. I went over to the house to stay the night, because Fred was afraid to be alone with her when she died. Too bad I didn't recognize this fear a little earlier. I may have minimized his fear, because Susan remained active, even driving until last week. We all have been into denial a bit. Just two nights ago she walked out to the living room and gave me a framed picture from her office wall. We talked with her last night about what she wanted me to get for Fred for Christmas. You know, she never did take any pain medicine—a little valium last night, but that was all. She died just as our first winter ice storm was moving in. The mortician wouldn't believe that I was staying over at the house when I called him last night. "Are you sure you're a doctor?" he asked. Was it that I was a woman, or was it that I was at a patient's house in the night that surprised him? When they came to get her body, her dog Custer wouldn't let them take her away. We had to hold Custer's collar as the undertaker rolled Susan on the cart through the house. Poor dog. Poor Susan. Poor Fred. Poor me. We are going back to the house later today to plan Susan's service with Fred. This seems so hard. Yet I am glad I took care of her, in spite of what my colleagues said. It has been one of the richest professional and personal experiences of my life.

October 1987

> How hard it is to escape from places!
> However carefully one goes, they hold you—
> you leave little bits of yourself
> fluttering on the fences, little rags
> and shreds of your very life.
>
> —Katherine Mansfield (1992, 183)

A friend called me today. She invited me for lunch, and I told her that I was too busy right now. Actually, I rarely eat lunch. She told me I always seemed too busy, not only for lunch, but for friendship. Several of my friends have made this charge recently, although most are gentle, and appear to be expressing their concern. Then there are patients who are upset because they can't get in to see me as quickly as they'd like. And there are my children, who should have the first hunk of my time. I wonder if there is supposed to be time for me, just for me. Novel thought. Maybe when the kids are grown.

I am tired. Tired of always having more people want things from me than I can possibly deliver. Tired of having people unhappy with me because I cannot give enough. My male colleagues all have wives to take care of their personal and social needs, take their suits to the cleaners, be at home when the plumber comes, go to the children's parent-teacher conferences, entertain at the appropriate intervals, go to the grocery store, buy the Christmas presents, maintain the friendships. I have no wife to do all this. I have a busy practice with no time to think about the solution. As I prioritize my time, patients and kids come first, necessities of life second, friends third, and myself last. The order may be incorrect, or at least out of balance. Or am I trying to keep too many people happy at once? Oh, how lovely it would be to have a wife.

July 1988, The Bargain

> She moves
> toward death the way a swimmer
> eases into freezing water:
> ankles, knees, hips,
> shivering ribcage, collarbone.
>
> —Lisel Mueller (1989, 37)

D.W. asked for sleeping pills today. I didn't have to ask her about sleep. It's been disrupted for years. By an unsatisfactory job, by too many bourbons, by feuds with friends and lovers, by searches in the night for shadows of meaning for her life. Now her sleep is interrupted by her efforts to take enough air into her scarred lungs. She knew Camels would do this. She watched both her father and mother die early deaths from lung cancer and emphysema. She has told me sixty is long enough to live. I have pleaded, challenged, bargained with her. Nicotine has had more influence than I.

Now she asks for sleeping pills. A lot of them. She wants to make sure, she says, that when it is too hard to breathe, she will have an easy exit. She doesn't want to suffocate. We bargain. I don't want to give her the pills, because I don't want to let her die alone. In exchange, I promise not to let her suffer. She agrees not to ask for sleeping pills. I agree to use morphine or valium or both, if needed, to make her comfortable. Even if it slows her breathing, or stops it perhaps. She says no hospitals. I agree to come to her house to care for her, along with a hospice nurse. The deal is cut.

Is this euthanasia? Or is it simply helping her be comfortable at the end of her disease? Does the Hippocratic Oath charge to "do no harm" fall on the side of doing too little or too much in this case? Can I tell my colleagues about this bargain? A heart attack would be welcome.

December 1988

> This above all, to refuse to be a victim.
> Unless I can do that I can do nothing.
>
> —Margaret Atwood (1972, 222)

It seems like the women on the faculty have two or three jobs. The men have one. The women see most of the patients, do most of the teaching, get half of the salary, and have little access to promotion or advancement of any type. When we complain, we are being "too negative." When we are tired, "it is your own fault." When we are overwhelmed, we "chose this bed." It is the same story I hear from my patients about their own lives day after day. A tale of being overworked, undervalued, underpaid, again invisible. Only when the work stops are we visible. We value relationships with our patients. We get blamed for getting too close. Subtly we are accused of being less efficient. When we write about public health/social conditions and single parenthood, it is discounted as "soft science." We do collaborative work with colleagues, and it doesn't count because it is not "sole authorship." We ask for humane working schedules, and we are considered "not tough enough." We ask for equal dressing rooms in the surgery suite; it is "being picky." The dressing rooms for male and female physicians, and male and female staff in surgery are divided into two areas. One is labelled "doctors," which is only for male physicians. The other is labelled "women," which excludes the male nurses. (I have yet to figure out where they dress.) Several of the women students complained, and were given lower evaluations by their attendings on surgery, all men. Is it coincidence?

I find myself increasingly torn between my own needs, the expectations of my job, the needs of my patients, and the needs of my children. Where is the balance? Where are the systems that are designed to protect health care workers, particularly the women? Margaret Atwood says, "Above all else, refuse to be a victim." In order not to be a victim, I must define my boundaries, and I must help the system change.

May 1989

> Don't know when I'll be back again . . .
>
> —John Denver (1970)

I am moving out of the only community I have known as a health care provider. It means leaving patients of twelve years, families I have come to love, with whom I have shared births, deaths, and many significant and insignificant moments. The job is a promotion to an administrative job, plus teaching and patient care. Everyone tells me it is a move up for my career. My heart only feels the incredible losses of leaving relationships that have helped to make me who I am, and have given me an understanding of how I am connected to those around me.

Although I will carry with me the memories, pictures, various gifts, and good wishes from patients, I am coming to understand that leaving these patients is permanent. In time the relationships will fade. The patients will move on to new doctors, I to new patients. The conversations I have had in the past few weeks echo in my head, across the highways and airline trails in the sky.

"How could you leave? I need you here."

"But you're the only doctor I ever liked.."

"I'll never go to the doctor again . . ."

"What's so hot about Michigan, anyway?"

"But my baby isn't due until September."

"Can I write you?"

The questions I have asked myself have been even harder:

How can I betray this trust I have taken so seriously?

How can I leave patients with terminal illnesses–those that are counting on me to lead them through the main exit?

How is it that my career is more important than the welfare of these people who have trusted me for twelve years?

How do I tell them? What do I tell them?

Why is it that I made this decision anyway?

June 1989

> This is the Hour of Lead–
> Remembered, if outlived,
> As Freezing persons, recollect the Snow–
> First-Chill-then Stupor-then the letting go-
>
> —Emily Dickinson (1890, 222)

As time gets closer, I find myself bargaining, saying that I will probably not like Michigan, and will come back. I listen as staff arrange appointments for my patients with other doctors. Secretly, I enjoy hearing that the replacements are not adequate. I'm not ready to be replaced. I don't like being invisible when I can still hear and see. I don't want these patients whom I have loved to forget me. I find myself looking for ways to change my mind, to call Michigan and tell them I'm not coming. I decide I don't want to move at all, I want to stay here with my practice. The Kansas sky, the wheatfields at harvest, the phlox and roses in my backyard, the patients, all have become too beautiful to leave. A piece of me is dying. This is what grief is.

February 1991

> When women, for example, are included in token numbers in group life–
> medical school, say, or the military–they are viewed not as individuals,
> but as representatives of their kind . . . The pressure to be 'tough as the
> boys' and to avoid doing anything out of line make it difficult to support or
> identify with other women.
>
> —Harriet Lerner (1993, 203)

Harriet Goldhor Lerner writes in her book, *Dance of Deception*, about tokenism, and its effect on those who are the tokens. I have become a token as a woman in an administrative position in a medical school. Often I find myself the only woman in meetings of ten to fifteen men. Rosabeth Kanter points out in her work on tokenism that women in these positions have to work harder, do better, to maintain credibility, to have influence. It certainly matches my experience. The cracking of glass ceilings, it seems, is inaudible, and leaves no glass on the floor as a reminder. At least yet. More than in medical school, I find myself aware of how invisible I seem to be while speaking up and clearly present in the same room. On other days, I find myself assigning myself too much visibility, aware of the care with which I frame my position and challenge the status quo. I wonder if I have been co-opted by the patriarchal rules of this institution, rules which go unchallenged. As Lerner points out, tokens often "underline, rather than undermine" (Lerner 1993, 202) the position of the majority, because of their tenuous position, and that they(we) "protect, rather than protest, the status quo (Lerner 1993, 203)."

It appears that in committees where there are only one or two women, the presence of a woman is acknowledged, but her competencies remain invisible. I notice that I make a point, clearly I believe, only to have a male colleague make the same point ten minutes later, with the support of his peers. Did I not just say the same thing? Are these doctors deaf? What is it that is going on here? At what point is it worth my time and energy to confront what is happening? It is the same struggle I experienced in medical school: when do I remain silent? When do I speak? I long for other women in these meetings. There are only two women in administrative positions in the medical school. We are never in the same meetings together. Always alone. Always simultaneously too visible and invisible. We are apparitions, I must conclude, like shadows cast on the water by sun and cloud. Wizards that appear and disappear at a moment's notice.

September 1992: Delivery

> Babies should grow in fields;
> common as beets or turnips
> they should be picked and held
> root end up, soil spilling
> from between their toes—
>
> —Linda Pastan (1993, 77)

So much for bragging. I was just telling one of the residents a couple weeks ago that, in over 2000 deliveries, I had never missed a set of twins. That good clinical assessment almost always identifies a multiple gestation. So, today at four in the morning (my usual time for deliveries) Mrs. K comes in with labor pains, expecting her third baby. She is two days away from her delivery date, has grown exactly as one would expect for a single baby, and thought this baby was the same size as her last one, about nine pounds. The only thing unusual about the pregnancy was that she has complained about being much more tired than with her other pregnancies. Well, she is 34, she has two preschoolers orbiting the house, and it has been a hot summer. Those explanations satisfied both of us.

The labor is short, and uneventful. Then out pops a baby. A small baby, not over six pounds I guess as I take it to the warmer. I was sure she would have a bigger baby than that. Then I look at her. She still had a rather large abdomen. I touch her, then listen for another heartbeat. Sure enough. 140. Then I check to see which way the next baby is coming. There is no one else around to help. Head first, thank God for small favors! I tell her she is going to have two babies, not one. The husband doesn't believe me. He argues with me that I couldn't be right. At this point, humility is in order, so I simply keep on with the work at hand and don't dispute his contentions. When the second boy comes out, the husband laughs, saying "I guess this ends our argument about whether to have three or four children." Both babies are five and a half pounds, both healthy. Their total weight is just over ten pounds. Only a pound off, if I am still into being confident in my clinical skills. So much for never missing twins. So much for being right.

July 1993: Meetings away from home

> You must look as if you're working,
> not playing.
>
> —Bernadine Morris (1978, 151)

I'm at a national meeting, sitting at the end of a row, listening to a talk, reading the program, and writing in my journal all simultaneously. I have learned over the years to do three things at once, and wonder what it would be like to only do one thing at a time. I might be bored, or I might be relaxed. Around the room I see other women, too few of them, some juggling babies on their hips while they stand in the back of the room, others doing needlework, others eating while they listen. Most of the men are just listening.

The clothes people wear on the first day of this conference are not suited for comfortable listening. It appears as if there is a dress code: slacks, shirts and ties, with black or brown shoes for the men; dresses or suits, stockings, pumps and makeup (tastefully applied) for the women. If past experience holds true, by tomorrow there will be a few people who dress for comfort, rather than fashion, and by the last day of the meeting, fully twenty-five percent of people will not be dressing according to "code."

Other issues get my attention as well. The speaker is a white male, using military metaphors to discuss the changes in medicine and in our specialty. They are metaphors that I don't understand or for which I have no sympathy. War *impedes* health, it seems to me. All of the folks on the platform are men; most of the people in the back of the room are women. We make it hard for women to feel comfortable at these meetings, particularly those with children, or those who are young and saddled with educational debt. The hotel costs $150 a night; the registration is $400; travel, and meals, and the meeting cost easily $1200 to $1500. There is little child care available, other than a hired stranger to sit with children in a hotel room. All of the awards this year go to men. All of the plenary speakers are men. Most of the officials in the organization are men. Forty-five percent of the audience is women. The few women who are in leadership appear to play very restricted roles. Suits and heels for dress, submissive demeanor, makeup, no children on hips, no questions about military metaphors. These women have been well trained in the rules of organizations and meetings. To dissent would mean lack of respect for the men in leadership. I should go out and take a walk. A hike. But I'm not dressed for it.

July 1994

> This is the place
> you would rather not know about,
> this is the place that will inhabit you,
> this is the place you cannot imagine,
> this is the place that will finally defeat you
> where the word "why" shrivels and empties
> itself. This is famine.
>
> —Margaret Atwood (1981, 65)

I cannot watch T.V. anymore. The pictures of the suffering, starving children on the nightly news, of the war, disease, and famine take away my comfortable evening interlude at the end of the day. I keep wondering what I should do. The newscaster tonight talked about twenty thousand people for every doctor, amid the cholera. Why don't I go help? What am I doing taking care of problems that are not life threatening, while I could be helping so much more? What is my responsibility in the face of public health disasters? What limits me from moving? I convince myself daily that it is not me they need, it is clean water. That I have little to offer. I am afraid to go, to leave the comforts of home, if the truth be known. I might well be killed, or die from unclean water myself. It is times such as these that I rail against ordering MRI's to reassure patients their migraine headaches are not terminal, while the same $800 would immunize more than a hundred children. I am complicitous in this unjust distribution of access to medical resources. Perhaps that is why watching the news hurts my eyes and my conscience.

August 1994: Letter to my student

> We forget all too soon the things we
> thought we could never forget.

> —Joan Didion (1990, 139)

"Is it possible to have it all?" you asked in our conversation earlier this week. I've thought about that some more. This certainly is an issue I have struggled with much of my career, particularly the tension between the responsibilities of parenthood and one's professional role.

Some of the things you bring to the profession because of your gender, and socialization as a woman, will make your work life both harder and easier. Again I go back to the writing of Harriet Lerner, who first pointed out for me in a way that I understood, how often women take care of others at the expense of themselves. Sometimes you will be up all night with a woman in labor, instead of snoozing in the call room down the hall; or you will go the extra mile, and do a home visit on an elderly patient, both to make it easier for her, and to see the home where the family lives in order to understand the caregiving situation better. You will do this with ease, because of your socialization.

On the other hand, occasionally you will work in the extra patient once too often, miss your child's soccer game because you said "yes" to a patient, cover for a colleague instead of going to the art fair. Then, your inbreeding as a woman will cause you difficulty. Your patients will love you for it. Your male colleagues will occasionally be suspicious and resentful of your popularity. The stacks of presents from grateful patients may be a barometer of how big this struggle is for you. Ultimately you must find your own set of rules, your own boundaries between responsibility and self care, your own understanding of how you fit into this role you have accepted. The zen diagram of your many roles (friend, mother, partner, physician, self) changes from day to day and year to year. Only you can determine where, for you, the lines overlap and where they cannot. You must pay attention to where one circle is getting too big, overshadowing others. Be thoughtful about it. Find mentors and trusted friends with whom you can discuss these issues on an ongoing basis. Your patients, also, will be good teachers if you listen to what they tell you. Write in your journal. Keep a log of your time. Keep a journal of your stories. They are the vitamins which will help you grow as a person and as a professional. These stories are also a roadmap of where you have been and where you are going. They are the accounting of how much of the "all" you have, and how much you really want.

I wish you peace.

CHAPTER 16

Special Armor

❏

Marjorie S. Sirridge

Recently I ordered for one of my granddaughters a T-shirt on which was printed *Girls Can Do Anything*. This was followed by a long list of careers from which girls might choose. I was surprised (and disappointed) that the list did not include medical doctors, thinking this career would be especially impor-tant to her since she had recently announced that she was going to be a cancer doctor. I was aware that this decision came about when a school friend's mother died suddenly of breast cancer, but I also knew that it was not entirely a new decision since she had asked for a "doctor kit" for Christmas two years ago. I'd like to think that my being a doctor had something to do with the decision, but I'm not so sure.

All of this made me think about how I might better connect with her, but it also sent me back to my own decision to become a doctor over fifty years ago. I didn't have a grandmother who was a doctor, and I certainly didn't have a T-shirt to suggest that I had lots of careers to choose from. Nor was there a feminist movement to encourage me to look beyond traditional jobs held by most of the women I knew. My mother and two aunts were teachers and seemed happy and satisfied in their work, so being a teacher would have been an acceptable choice. An uncle who was a lawyer told me that women didn't make good lawyers, and I accepted that as truth even though I didn't understand why. Fortunately no one told me that women didn't make good doctors, and practicing medicine certainly sounded more interesting and novel than teaching school. I was amazed that the choice seemed quite acceptable to many of the people I knew, and once I announced the decision publicly, I found I was stuck with it. Yet my dedication to my new goal grew, and I found that I enjoyed the challenge of defending my choice. It made me feel special and amazingly enough, I still do. Even now when I'm filling out a form which requires me to state my occupation, I always feel proud to write physician. What a wonderful armor this feeling has provided over the years, and how well it prepared me to expect and accept a certain amount of discrimination.

As I reflect back on my life as a pre-medical student, I believe it went smoothly mainly because I was a strong student and did well in the required preparatory subjects for medical school. I was, however, the only female pre-medical student in my college class of well over a thousand students, and I received no encouragement or help from either teachers or peers. But I was inspired by reading the autobiography of a very successful woman surgeon, a book given to me by my parents, which I saw as evidence of their support. I also found my first real role-model, a young woman physician who was on the staff of the university student health service.

Dr. Ruth Montgomery-Short was the first woman I knew who had chosen to hyphenate her name after marriage. She was only in her first year of practice after completing a one-year internship, but to me she seemed wonderfully accomplished as a physician. She was a very practical, serious person and was working at the college because her husband was in veterinary school there. She performed my admission physical examination (much to my relief) and later wrote medical school recommendations for me. She assured me that medical school wouldn't present any insurmountable problems for me as a woman. Later I came to understand that her being a wife and later the mother of three daughters certainly did present problems and did shape her career as similar experiences have shaped mine. We have remained friends since that encounter long ago and can now laugh at our naiveté and the incongruity of our lives as women and physicians.

Even though admission interviews for medical school were somewhat harrowing, my admission to medical school came as no surprise to me. I knew that I had done exceedingly well on the MCAT and I knew that I deserved to be admitted. Interviewers kept suggesting to me that medicine was not really a good choice for a woman, but I was developing my armor to protect me and I accepted such comments as challenges. The school accepted five women that year, which was surprising since the only woman selected the year before had dropped out. I was thankful that I would have women peers in this adventure.

During the preclinical years, I saw little difference in the way the women were treated by a faculty composed mainly of men. It was much like being an undergraduate, except that we were much more isolated in many ways. The men gathered into three medical fraternities, which provided not only friendly, congenial living situations but also a shared study and learning experience. Their quiz files were a luxury the women didn't have. The little band of women, too often referred to as "hen medics," studied together and provided emotional support for each other. We all passed, and I managed to stay at the top of the class, a position that further strengthened my armor. No one mentioned my academic success, including myself, but I think the other women students were proud of me.

Two older women joined us later, one who had completed a Ph.D. and another who had dropped out of school a few years before when her first child was born. But even though women now comprised eight percent of the class, we continued to feel isolated, a condition which was exacerbated during the clinical years. Many of the clinicians and hospital personnel didn't view us as serious aspirants to physicianhood. There were always a few faculty members who found it necessary to try to embarrass women, but this was better than being ignored during clinical discussions, which also occurred. On-call quarters for men were limited but they were nonexistent for women. There were many chinks in my armor during this period.

World War II started while I was in medical school, which produced a shortage of interns and externs. I was able to work every other evening as an extern in a private Catholic hospital during my last year in medical school. The male hierarchical system was less powerful in this hospital, and I was treated with a great deal more respect. This was a real confidence building experience and helped prepare me for my rotating internship in a much larger public hospital.

Like two other women in my class, I married a man from our class. We were married the day before graduation, and then began to serve internships in hospitals separated by thousands of miles. There seemed to be little gender discrimination for interns at either hospital probably because the work load was so heavy and everyone felt overworked equally. The percentage of women was small and there were no women residents on surgical services. As interns, however, women were assigned to all services and were expected to assume all types of responsibilities. Women's quarters were poor and inconvenient, but I don't remember much complaining about it. We expected it and accepted it since we were the invaders in a male-dominated hospital world. We felt that we were privileged to be there and most of us were exceptionally hard workers and overachievers. I don't think we saw ourselves as different, just as interns. Doing a good job paid off in satisfaction and sometimes in an opportunity for a choice residency position, except, of course, in specialties reserved for men.

The real difference for me because of my gender began when I became pregnant in my first year of residency and realized that I was not going to be free to be "one of the boys." I had never known a pregnant resident and I asked myself how I could provide care for a child and continue my training. The answer was, at that time and under those circumstances, I couldn't. I had to admit that my life as a physician was going to be different from the lives of my male colleagues. And it has been different ever since. I don't think I realized the *universality* of this awareness until my daughter, a philosophy professor, said to me, "After the birth of your first child, you are never ever again free."

So I dropped out of the training program after I had completed only half of the required time. The birth of two more children very quickly left me with little hope that I could soon get back into the mainstream. Fortunately five years later my husband (whose training had not been interrupted) was making enough money in his medical practice to allow us to hire someone to care for the children during the day. The bigger hurdle was to find a training program in our area which would accept a woman with my time limitations. After many unsuccessful efforts I found a friendly hospital pathologist who offered me the opportunity to work a daytime schedule with him, a lot like the old apprenticeship tradition in medicine. He was an excellent teacher and gave me a great deal of responsibility, so learning proceeded at an accelerated pace during that year. Of course I received no salary and no official credit. Still, I arranged a second unofficial year at the university hospital of the medical school from which I had been graduated eight years before, only to experience another delay when my husband was called into the armed forces and I became pregnant for the fourth time.

Finally, two years later, I joined my husband in setting up a joint practice. Fortunately I had the skills and special training in hematology which was needed in our medical community and in the medical school curriculum, so I was not only successful in practice but became active as a member of the clinical teaching faculty at the medical school. Being a woman was not a significant problem, but the lack of orthodox training kept me from achieving appropriate certification as a specialist. I saw this as a professional disadvantage, and in spite of my armor, it left me with a feeling of inferiority. Not only was I not an "old boy," but I didn't even have official membership in the club. I knew I had the qualifications (if not the official ones that really mattered) but I knew that those weren't good enough for the medical community, and subsequently, not for me.

So I worked harder and became even more of an overachiever. I already had the major responsibilities for home and children, and to that I added on the management responsibilities at the office of our private practice. As if that weren't enough, I wrote several journal articles and a single-authored medical textbook entitled *Laboratory Evaluation of Hemostasis*. The opportunity to write the book had come through the efforts of a woman friend who appreciated the way in which I had helped medical technologists understand the complex processes involved in blood clotting. My own interest and research in this area had started during my second year of postgraduate training and had continued after I started practicing. Such information was much needed because of the lack of understanding of bleeding disorders and of ways to care for patients who suffered from them. I became a local authority and was also asked to speak at national meetings on the subject.

I did the writing for the textbook alone, expecting and receiving no support from faculty and staff of the medical school where I served on the clinical faculty. In spite of the extent of this work, I was very gratified to accomplish this *on my own.* Fortunately, the book sold well, but more with medical technologists, who are mostly female, than with physicians, who are mostly male. Probably one of my most uncomfortable memories was a comment made by a somewhat haughty male hematologist who, when introduced to me, said, "Oh, you're the woman who wrote the hemostasis cookbook." Still, I knew that he could not have done what I had done, despite his more powerful position and his support from "the guys." Also, he was using the cookbook.

In spite of this success and years in practice that brought many rewards from patients, I still had the desire to become a full-time medical school faculty member and to prove that, as a woman physician, I had academic capabilities equal to my male colleagues. The opportunity to move in that direction and also to take on a new challenge came with the opening of a new and innovative medical school in our city just over twenty-five years ago. It was easy to be an equal partner in the early development of this school as the work and energy required were vast, just as they had been in my internship year. However, as the school grew and matured it became obvious that the usual male hierarchical system was going to prevail, and so it has: the power remains in the hands of men, and women continue to be primarily in secondary positions.

As the senior woman faculty member in this school I have, from the beginning, been intensely involved in issues related to women students. It has been relatively easy to bring attention to physicians who abuse and harass women students in obvious ways, even though less overt abuse goes unreported on many clinical rotations. There has always been, however, covert discrimination in the ways learning opportunities are made available to women and men. Despite their equal numbers to men, many women are uncomfortable when they feel they must utilize aggressive tactics to be taken seriously. I must confess that I have felt disappointed that increased numbers of women have not given women the confidence they need to participate fully and equally with men in the process of their medical education. As their teacher I see women speak out less often and ask fewer questions. I say this with the knowledge that teachers instinctively give more attention to male students than to women students. But I wonder: is it that men *demand* more attention? If so, I want women students to learn how to be more comfortable making the same demands.

Sadly, I have come to realize that many of today's women medical students expect and accept discrimination in much the same way the small band of women with whom I started to medical school did. The role of a female faculty member today is different from that of the few women who taught me many years ago. Not only were they few in number but none had positions of power or influence. I don't remember a single woman during my medical school and postgraduate training years who was important to me as a role model or mentor. Certainly today there are increased numbers of women and they are usually quite visible to students as role models. Also they sometimes have opportunities to be mentors though all are not comfortable in this role. My reputation has been that of one who speaks out for myself and for women, and both male and female students have told me that my influence here has been a positive one for women students. I always feel honored when students come to talk with me about their lives and their goals. Both men and women have sought advice about dual career marriages, and women particularly have wanted to talk about combining a career and family life. It is indeed a challenge to be a good role model as a physician and teacher and also to be available as a friendly counselor.

One of the good things which has come about in medical education is the emphasis on a different kind of attention to women's health issues. This is due to the work of feminist scientists, physicians, health care providers, and perhaps even more to the demands of women patients themselves. Increased numbers of women physicians have also made a difference, and women patients have learned that they can often expect more understanding from women physicians for many of their health problems. Thus the availability of more women physicians and the demands of women patients have together made the previously male-dominated specialty of obstetrics and gynecology more open to women. This trend should continue, and though women still choose primary care specialties more often than men, many are ready to venture into other male-dominated specialties like surgery and orthopedics. But it is unlikely that they will find warm welcomes.

For myself, I can look back and see my decision to become a physician as a pioneering one, and the decision to help establish a new medical school in much the same way. Both these decisions were rewarding in many ways, but both extracted tolls. More recently I have undertaken a new pioneering effort in teaching courses in literature and medicine and helping to develop an Office of Medical Humanities at our medical school. (My daughter calls it my third career.) I have embraced it just as I did medicine, because of my genuine interest in the subject and also because of my urge to do something different and special. This endeavor has not, however, required the special armor I have worn before, because it isn't a male-dominated field and, at least now, it is peopled mainly with persons, regardless of their gender, who have genuine concern for human beings who are suffering and for those who care for them. I have not noticed urges for power and authority in this field, urges I always felt were present in the clinical practice of medicine. This has allowed me to re-examine my own beliefs and motivations surrounding medicine and to speak more openly with medical students as we study literature together. More remarkably, it has allowed me to feel lighter, and freer, more myself . . . not weighted down by armor.

References

Introduction

Haraway, D. 1988. Situated knowledges: The science question in feminism and the privilege of partial perspective. *Feminist Studies*, 14(3):575-599.

Harding, S. 1986. *The science question in feminism.* Ithaca: Cornell University Press.

hooks, b. 1992, July/August. Out of the academy and into the streets. *Ms.*:80-82.

Lather, P. 1991. *Getting smart: Feminist research and pedagogy with/in the postmodern.* New York: Routledge.

Miller, N. K. 1991. *Getting personal: Feminist occasions and other autobiographical acts.* New York: Routledge.

Sherwin, S. 1992. Feminist and medical ethics: Two different approaches to contextual ethics. In *Feminist perspectives in medical ethics*, eds. H. Holmes and L. Purdy, 17-31. Bloomington, IN: Indiana University Press.

Walsh, M. R. 1979. The rediscovery of the need for a feminist medical education. *Harvard Educational Review* 49:447-466.

Warren, V. L. 1992. Feminist directions in medical ethics. In *Feminist perspectives in medical ethics*, eds. H. Holmes and L. Purdy, 32-45. Bloomington, IN: Indiana University Press.

Yeatman, A. 1994. Postmodern epistemological politics and social science. In *Knowing the difference: Feminist perspectives in epistemology*, eds. K. Lennon and M. Whitford, 187-274. London: Routledge.

Chapter 1

Association of American Medical Colleges. 1995, March 2. Memorandum #95-11. Washington, D.C.

Bickel, J., A. Galbraith, and R. Quinnie. 1995. *Women in U.S. academic medicine statistics.* Washington, D.C.: Association of American Medical Colleges.

Council on Graduate Medical Education. 1995. Fifth report: Women and medicine. Bethesda, MD: Department of Health and Human Services.

Dickstein, L. J. 1991. The ceiling: Is it of breakable glass or unbreakable lexan? *Psychiatric News* 26(24):19.

Drachman, V. 1984. *Hospital with a heart: Women doctors and the paradox of separatism at the New England Hospital, 1862–1969*. Ithaca: Cornell University Press.

Flexner, A. 1910. *Medical administration in the United States*. New York: Carnegie Foundation.

Lenhart, S. 1993. Gender discrimination: A health and career development problem for women physicians. *Journal of the American Medical Women's Association* 48:1155.

Morantz-Sanchez, R. 1985. *Sympathy and science: Women physicians in American medicine*. New York: Oxford University Press.

Ouchterlony, J. A. 1890. Pioneer physicians and surgeons in Kentucky: The presidential address. *The Medical Progress* 4 (June):838–39.

Robinson, M. 1991, October. Keynote lecture commemorating 100 years of women at Brown. Providence, RI: Brown University.

Walsh, M. R. 1977. *Physicians wanted: No women need apply*. New Haven: Yale University Press.

Women add a new dimension to medicine. 1995, March. *The New Physician* [special issue].

Chapter 2

Barreca, R. 1991. *They used to call me Snow White . . . But I drifted: Women's strategic use of humor*. New York: Penguin Books.

Benocraitis, N. V. and J. R. Feagin. 1986. *Modern sexism: Blatant, subtle and covert discrimination*, 13–20. Englewood Cliffs, NJ: Prentiss Hall.

Bergman, S. J. and J. Surrey. 1993. The changing nature of relationships on campus: Impasses and possibilities. *Educational Record* 74(1):13–20.

Bickel, J. 1994. Women as leaders in academic medicine. In *Taking care: The changing roles of women in health care*, ed. E. Friedman. New York: United Hospital Fund.

Bickel, J. 1995. Scenarios for success: Enhancing women physicians' professional advancement. *Western Journal of Medicine* 162:165–69.

Bickel, J. and G. Povar. 1995. Women as health professionals: Contemporary issues. In *The Encyclopedia of Bioethics*, revised edition, ed. W. Reich, 2585-91. New York: Macmillan Publishing.

Bickel, J. and R. Quinnie. 1995. *Women in U.S. academic medicine statistics.* Washington, D.C.: Association of American Medical Colleges.

Case, S. 1990. Communication styles in higher education: Differences between academic men and women. In *Women in higher education: Changes and challenges*, ed. L. Welch. New York: Praeger.

Dresselhaus, M. S., J. R. Franz, and B. C. Clark. 1994. Interventions to increase the participation of women in physics. *Science* 263:1392-3.

Fiske, S. 1993. Controlling other people: The impact of power on stereotyping. *American Psychologist* 48:621-8.

Fletcher, S. and R. Fletcher. 1993. Here come the couples. *Annals of Internal Medicine* 119:628-30.

Franco, K. et al. 1993. Letter to the editor: Experience with pregnant physicians has been a good teacher. *Academic Medicine* 68:206.

Froom, J. and J. Bickel. 1996. Medical school policies for part-time faculty committed to full professional effort. *Academic Medicine* 71:91-96.

Grisso, J. A., L. Hansen, I. Zelling, J. Bickel, and J. M. Eisenberg. 1991. Parental leave policies for faculty in U.S. medical schools. *Annals of Internal Medicine* 114:43-45.

Hostler, S. L. and R. P. Gressard. 1993. Perceptions of the gender fairness of the medical education environment. *Journal of the American Medical Women's Association* 48:51-54.

Jeruchim, J. and J. Shapiro. 1992. *Women, mentors, and success.* New York: Ballantine Books.

Kanter, R. M. 1977. *Men and women of the corporation.* New York: Basic Books.

Korn/Ferry International. 1993. *Decade of the executive women, 1982-1992.* New York: Korn/Ferry International.

Koshland, D. E. 1993. Women in science. *Science* 261:1326.

Lenhart, S. and C. Evans. 1991. Sexual harassment and gender discrimination: A primer for women physicians. *Journal of the American Medical Women's Association* 46:77-82.

Levinson, W., K. Kaufman, and J. Bickel. 1993. Part-time faculty in academic medicine: Present status and future challenges. *Annals of Internal Medicine* 119: 220-225.

Menand, L. 1993, May-June. The future of academic freedom. *Academe*:11-17.

Morrison, A. M., R. P. White, and E. Van Velson. 1987, August. Executive women: Substance plus style. *Psychology Today*:18-26.

Moscarello, R., K. J. Margittai, and M. Rossi. 1994. Difference in abuse reported by female and male Canadian medical students. *Canadian Medical Association Journal* 150:357-363.

Mossberg, B. 1993. Chaos on campus: A prescription for global leadership. *Educational Record* 74(4):49-54.

Ragins, B. R. and E. Sundstrom. 1989. Gender and power in organizations: A longitudinal perspective. *Psychological Bulletin* 105:51-88.

Stobo, J. D., L. P. Fried, and E. J. Stokes. 1993. Understanding and eradicating bias against women in medicine. *Academic Medicine* 68:349.

Tesch, B. and A. B. Nattinger. 1994. Creative part-time faculty arrangements (correspondence). *Annals of Internal Medicine* 120:346.

Westberg, J. and H. Jason. 1996. *Fostering learning in small groups: A practical guide.* New York: Springer Publishing

Wheatley, M. 1992. *Leadership and the new science: Learning about organization from an orderly universe.* San Francisco: Berret-Koehler Publishers.

Chapter 3

Bickel, J. and R. Quinnie. 1993. *Building a stronger women's program: Enhancing the professional and educational environments.* Washington, D.C.: Association of American Medical Colleges.

Bickel, J. 1994. Special needs and affinities of women medical students. In *The empathic practitioner: Empathy, gender and medicine,* ed. E. More. New Brunswick, NJ: Rutgers University Press.

Chapter 4

Bonner, T. N. 1992. *To the ends of the earth: Women's search for education in medicine.* Cambridge, MA: Harvard University Press.

Dodd, D. and D. Gorham. 1994. *Caring and curing.* Ottawa: University of Ottawa Press.

Drachman, V. G. 1976. *Women doctors and the women's medical movement: Feminism and medicine, 1850-1895.* Ann Arbor, MI: University Microfilms.

Drachman, V. G. 1986. Women doctors and the quest for professional power, 1881-1926. In *Women physicians in leadership roles,* eds. L. Dickstein and C. Nadelson, 3-12. Washington, D. C.: American Psychiatric Press.

Duffin, J. 1995. Infiltrating the curriculum: An integrative approach to history for medical students. *Journal of Medical Humanities* 16:155–174.

Fryer, M. B. 1990. *Emily Stowe: Doctor and suffragist.* Toronto: Dundurn Press and The Hannah Institute for the History of Medicine.

Gorham, D. 1976. The Canadian suffragist. In *Women in the Canadian mosaic*, ed. G. Matheson, 23–55. Toronto: Clarke Irwin.

Hacker, C. 1974. *The indomitable lady doctors.* Toronto: Clarke Irwin.

Lorber, J. 1984. *Women physicians: Career, status, and power.* New York: Tavistock Publications.

Morantz-Sanchez, R. 1985. *Sympathy and science: Women physicians in American medicine.* New York: Oxford University Press.

Strong-Boag, V. 1979. Canada's women doctors: Feminism constrained. In *A not unreasonable claim*, ed. L. Kealey. Toronto: The Women's Press.

Walsh, M. R. 1977. *Doctors wanted: No women need apply.* New Haven: Yale University Press.

Chapter 5

de Beauvoir, S. 1952. *The second sex.* New York: Bantam Books.

Deegan, M. F. 1988. *Jane Addams and the men of the Chicago school, 1892–1918.* New Brunswick, NJ: Transaction, Inc.

Gilligan, C. 1987. Moral orientation and moral development. In *Women and moral theory*, eds. E. F. Kittay and D. T. Meyers. Totawa, NJ: Rowman and Littlefield.

Hartshorne, C. and P. Weiss, eds. 1974. *Collected papers of Charles Sanders Peirce*, vol. 1. Cambridge, MA: The Belknap Press of Harvard University Press.

James, W. 1965. *Pragmatism.* New York: World Publishing Co.

Jonsen, A. 1987. On being a casuist. In *Clinical medical ethics*, eds. G. Graber, C. H. Reynolds, and D. Thomasma, 117–129. Lanham, MD: University Press of America.

Mahowald, M. B. 1987. A majority perspective: Feminine and feminist elements in American philosophy. *Cross Currents* 36:410–17.

Mahowald, M. B. 1992. A pregnant fellow. Case study for *The Hastings Center Report* 22:30–31.

Mahowald, M. B. 1993. Collaboration and casuistry: A Peircian pragmatic for the clinical setting. In *Peirce and value theory: On Peircian ethics and aesthetics*, ed. H. Parrot, 61–71. Amsterdam/Philadelphia: John Benjamins Publishing House.

Mahowald, M. B. 1972. *An idealistic pragmatism*. The Hague: Nijhoff.

Mahowald, M. B. [1978, 1983] 1994. *The philosophy of woman*. Indianapolis: Hackett Publishing Co.

Mahowald, M. B. 1993. *Women and children in health care: An unequal majority*. New York: Oxford University Press.

McDermott, J. J. 1973. *The philosophy of John Dewey*. New York: G. P. Putnam's Sons.

McLanahan, S. S., A. Spenser, and D. Watson. 1989. Sex differentiation poverty, 1950-1980. *Signs: Journal of Women in Culture and Society* 15:102-155.

Merriam-Webster's collegiate dictionary, 10th ed. 1993. Springfield, MA: Merriam-Webster, Inc.

Navarro, V. 1990. Women in health care. *International Journal of Health Services* 20:398-402.

Noddings, N. 1984. *Caring: A feminine approach to ethics and moral education*. Berkeley: University of California Press.

Okin, S. 1989. *Justice, gender, and the family*. New York: Basic Books.

Pearce, D. 1978. The feminization of poverty: Women, work and welfare. *Urban and Social Change Review* 11:23-36.

Royce, J. [1899] 1959. *The world and the individual, 1*. New York: Dover Publications.

Ruddick, S. 1984. Maternal thinking. In *Mothering*, ed. J. Trebilcot. Totowa, NJ: Rowman and Littlefield Publishers.

Sherwin, S. 1992. *No longer patient: Feminist ethics and health care*. Philadelphia: Temple University Press.

Sidel, R. 1989. *Women and children last*. New York: Basic Books.

Thayer, H. S. 1981. *Meaning and action: A critical history of pragmatism*. Indianapolis: Hackett Publishing Co.

Weaver, J. 1978. Sexism and racism in the American health care industry: A comparative analysis. *International Journal of Health Services* 8:677-700.

West, C. 1989. *The American evasion of philosophy: A genealogy of pragmatism*. Madison: University of Wisconsin Press.

Wiener, P. 1966. *Charles S. Peirce: Selected writings*. New York: Dover Publishing Co.

Chapter 6

Bernstein, A. and J. Cock. 1994, June 15. A troubling picture of gender equity. *The Chronicle of Higher Education*, B1-B3.

Bickel, J. and R. Quinnie. 1993. *Building a stronger women's program*. Washington, D.C.: Association of American Medical Colleges.

Conley, F. K. 1993. Toward a more perfect world–Eliminating sexual discrimination in academic medicine. *New England Journal of Medicine* 328:352.

Donegan, J. B. 1984. Safe delivered but by whom? Midwives and men-midwives in early America. In Leavitt, 302-317.

Ehrenreich, B. and D. English. 1978. *For her own good: 150 years of the experts' advice to women*. New York: Doubleday.

Fort, D. L., ed. 1993. *A hand up: Women mentoring women in science*. Washington, D.C.: Association for Women in Science.

Grant, C. A. and C. E. Sleeter. 1986. Race, class, and gender in educational research: An argument for an integrated analysis. *Review of Educational Research* 56(2):195-211.

Grosz, E. 1993. Philosophy. In *Feminist knowledge, critique and construct*. London: Routledge.

hooks, b. 1984. *Feminist theory from margin to center*. Boston: South End Press.

Jones, K. 1993. Perceptions of medical school: Not an entirely benign procedure. Unpublished manuscript.

Kaminer, W. 1993, October. Feminism's identity crisis. *The Atlantic Monthly*, 51-53, 56, 58-59, 62, 64, 66-68.

Leavitt, J. W. 1984. *Women and health in America*. Madison: University of Wisconsin Press.

Lorber, J. 1984. *Women physicians: Careers, status, and power*. New York: Tavistock Publications.

Lorber, J. 1993. Why women physicians will never be true equals in the American medical profession. In Riska, 62-76.

Marrett, C. B. 1984. On the evolution of women's medical societies. In Leavitt, 429-437.

Melosh, B. 1984. More than "the physician's hand": Skill and authority in twentieth century nursing. In Leavitt, 482-496.

Mies, M. 1983. Towards a methodology for feminist research. In *Theories of women's studies*, eds. G. Bowles and R. D. Klein, 117-139. London: Rutledge and Kegan Paul.

Mierson, S. and F. Chew. 1993. Dismantling internalized sexism. In Fort, 261-266.

Moldow, G. 1987. *Women doctors in gilded age Washington: Race, gender, and professionalization*. Urbana: University of Illinois Press.

Riggs, R. O., P. H. Murrell, and J. C. Cutting. 1993. Sexual harassment in higher education: From conflict to community. ASHE-ERIC Higher Education Report No. 2. Washington, D.C.: George Washington University.

Riska, E. and K. Wegar. 1993. *Gender, work and medicine.* Newbury Park, CA: Sage Publications.

Riska, E. and K. Wegar. 1993. Women physicians: A new force in medicine? In *Gender, work and medicine,* eds. E. Riska and K. Wegar. Newbury Park, CA: Sage Publications.

Rosser, S. V. 1990. *Female friendly science.* New York: Pergamon Press.

Scholten, C. M. 1984. On the importance of the obstetrick art: Changing customs of childbirth in America, 1760-1825. In Leavitt, 142-154.

Sherwin, S. 1992. *No longer patient: Feminist ethics and health care.* Philadelphia: Temple University Press.

Shyrock, R. H. 1950. Women in American medicine. *Journal of the American Medical Women's Association* 5(9):371-379.

Tobias, S. 1993. The problem of women in science: Why is it so difficult to convince people there is one? In Fort, 150-159.

Walsh, M. R. 1984. Feminist showplace. In Leavitt, 392-405.

Webster's New Riverside Dictionary. 1988. Boston: Houghton Mifflin Co.

Witz, A. 1993. *Professions and patriarchy.* London: Routledge.

Chapter 9

Belenky, M., B. Clinchy, N. Goldberger, and J. Tarule. 1986. *Women's ways of knowing.* New York: Basic Books.

Ferguson, K. W. 1984. *The feminist case against bureaucracy.* Philadelphia: Temple University Press.

Gilligan, C. 1982. *In a different voice.* Cambridge, MA: Harvard University Press.

Harding, S. 1991. *Whose science? Whose knowledge? Thinking from women's lives.* Ithaca, NY: Cornell University Press.

Ruddick, S. 1989. *Maternal thinking: Toward a politics of peace.* New York: Ballantine Books.

Sherwin, S. 1992. *No longer patient.* Philadelphia: Temple University Press.

Stone, L. 1994. *The education feminism reader.* New York: Routledge.

Tannen, D. 1993, June 20. Wears jump suit. Sensible shoes. Uses husband's last name. *The New York Times Magazine.*

Weiler, K. 1988. *Women teaching for change.* New York: Bergin and Garvey Publishers.

Chapter 10

Beverly, E. and W. Fox. 1989. Liberals must confront the conservative argument: Teaching humanities means teaching about values. *Chronicle of Higher Education* 36(9):52.

Bordo, S. 1990. Feminism, postmodernism, and gender-skepticism. In *Feminism/postmodernism,* ed. L. Nicholson, 133–156. New York: Routledge.

Messer-Davidow, E. 1989. The philosophical bases of feminist literary criticism. In *Gender and theory: Dialogues on feminist criticism,* ed. L. Kauffman, 63–106. Oxford: Basil Blackwell.

Greene, M. 1987. Sense-making through story: An autobiographical inquiry. *Teaching Education* 1(2):9–14.

Greene, M. 1988. *The dialectic of freedom.* New York: Teachers College Press.

Hennessy, R. 1993. *Materialist feminism and the politics of discourse.* New York: Routledge.

Hilfiker, D. 1989. *Facing brokenness. Second Opinion* 11:92–107.

Lather, P. 1991. *Getting smart: Feminist research and pedagogy with/in the postmodern.* New York: Routledge.

Lewis, M. and R. Simon, 1986. A discourse not intended for her: Learning and teaching within patriarchy. *Harvard Educational Review* 56:457–72.

Miller, N. K. 1991. *Getting personal: Feminist occasions and other autobiographical acts.* New York: Routledge.

Morrison, T. 1970. *The bluest eye.* New York: Simon and Schuster.

Olds, S. 1984. Miscarriage. In *The Dead and the Living,* 25. New York: Alfred A. Knopf.

Pastan, L. 1982. Notes from the delivery room. In *PM/AM: New and selected poems,* 26. New York: W. W. Norton.

Schweickart, P. 1986. Reading ourselves: Toward a feminist theory of reading. In *Gender and reading: Essays on readers, texts, and contexts,* ed. E. Flynn and P. Schweickart, 31–61. Baltimore: The Johns Hopkins University Press.

Tillman, L. 1991. Critical fiction/critical self. In *Critical fictions: The politics of imaginative writing,* ed. P. Mariani, 97–103. Seattle: Bay Press.

Chapter 12

hooks, b. 1994. *Teaching to transgress.* New York: Routledge.

Chapter 13

Friday, N. 1977. *My mother/myself.* New York: Delacorte Press.

Gilligan, C. 1982. *In a different voice.* Cambridge, MA: Harvard University Press.

Lum, C. K. and S. G. Korenman. 1994. Cultural sensitivity training in U. S. medical schools. *Academic Medicine* 69:239–241.

Chapter 14

Berger, J. and J. Mohr. 1976. *A fortunate man.* London: Writers and Readers Publishing Cooperative.

Bowman, M. A. and D. I. Allen. 1985. *Stress and women physicians.* New York: Springer-Verlag.

Brown, J. B. 1992. Female family doctors: Their work and wellbeing. *Family Medicine* 24:591–595.

Candib, L. M., S. L. Steinberg, J. Bedinhaus, M. Martin, R. Wheeler, M. Pugnaire, and R. Wertheimer. 1987. Doctors having families: The effect of pregnancy and child-bearing on relationships with patients. *Family Medicine* 19(2):114–119.

Cartwright, L. K. and P. Wink. 1994. Personality change in women physicians from medical student years to mid-40s. *Psychology of Women Quarterly* 18:291–308.

Kanter, R. M. 1977. *Men and women of the corporation.* New York: Basic Books.

Lorber, J. 1984. *Women physicians: Careers, status, and power.* New York: Tavistock Publications.

Scheman, N. 1993. *Engenderings: Constructions of knowledge, authority, and privilege.* New York: Routledge.

Wheeler, R., L. Candib, and M. Martin. 1990. Part-time doctors: Reduced working hours for primary care physicians. *Journal of the American Medical Women's Association* 45(2):47–54.

Chapter 15

Atwood, M. 1972. *Surfacing.* New York: Popular Library.

Atwood, M. 1981. Notes towards a poem that can never be written. *True stories,* 65. New York: Simon and Schuster.

Denver, J. 1970. From *The best of Peter, Paul, and Mary*. Warner Brothers.

Dickinson, E. [1890] 1927. *The complete poems of Emily Dickinson*. Boston: Little, Brown, and Co.

Didion, J. 1990. On keeping a notebook. In *Slouching toward Bethlehem*, 139. New York: Noonday Press.

Donne, J. 1990. Meditation XVIII. In *John Donne: A critical edition of major works*, ed. J. Carey, 344. New York: Oxford University Press.

Eliot, G. quoted in Sumrall, 38.

Forché, C. 1981. The visitor. In *The country between us*, 15. New York: Harper and Row.

Forché, C. 1981. Because one is always forgotten, 23. In *The country between us*. New York: Harper and Row.

Lerner, H. 1993. *Dance of deception*. New York: Harper Collins.

Mansfield, K. quoted in Sumrall, 183.

Morris, B. 1978, November. Self-confident dressing. *Harper's Bazaar*, 151.

Mueller, L. 1989. Mary. In *Waving from shore*, 37. Baton Rouge: Louisiana State University Press.

Pastan, L. 1993. Notes from the delivery room. In *Virago book of birth poetry*, ed. C. Otten, 77. London: Virago Press.

Plath, S. 1961. The applicant, 4. In *Ariel*. New York: Harper and Row.

Porter, I. quoted in Sumrall, 28.

Sand, G. quoted in Sumrall, 189.

Skeen, A. *Speaking in tongues*. Unpublished manuscript.

Sumrall, A., ed. 1992. *Write to the heart*. Freedom, CA: Crossing Press.

Thomas, D. [1952] 1976. Do not go gentle into that good night. In *Modern poems*, ed. R. Ellmann and R. O'Clair, 339. New York: W. W. Norton.

Walker, A. 1984. Remember? In *Horses make a landscape look more beautiful*, 1. New York: Harcourt Brace and Company.

Contributors

Beth Alexander is a Professor in the Department of Family Practice at Michigan State University. She teaches both medical students and residents, and her scholarly work is in the area of managed care, adolescence and human sexuality. She has won awards for Patient Education Materials, as a Distinguished Clinician and Teacher, and most recently as an ACE Fellow for Academic Leadership. Her most prized accomplishment is the delivery of 2200 babies during her still active clinical practice. Although still in mid-career, she was the first woman with children to be admitted to the University of Kansas School of Medicine in 1974.

Dale G. Blackstock graduated from Brooklyn College and Harvard Medical School. Her residency in medicine was at Harlem Hospital Center, and she completed a fellowship in nephrology at Brookdale Hospital Medical Center. She is an Assistant Professor in the Department of Medicine and Division of Nephrology at SUNY Health Science Center at Brooklyn and an attending at the Medical Clinic of Kings County Hospital Center in Brooklyn.

Deborah L. Jones is a Field Representative for the Accreditation Council for Graduate Medical Education. She has taught and conducted research in medical education for over twenty years. Her main teaching interests are literature and medicine and gender issues as they relate to health care. Her research includes work on the moral dimensions of advance directives and in developing models to teach empathetic curiosity.

Delese Wear is an Associate Professor of Behavioral Sciences and Associate Director of the Women in Medicine Program at the Northeastern Ohio Universities College of Medicine, where she also coordinates the Human Values in Medicine Program, which integrates the humanities into the study of medicine. She is editor of *The Center of the Web: Women and Solitude* (1993) and co-author of *Literary Anatomies: Women's Bodies and Health in Literature* (1994), both published by SUNY. Her interests include feminist criticism in the medical humanities, and feminist pedagogy/research methodologies.

Frances K. Conley is Professor of Neurosurgery at Stanford University Medical School and is Chief, Neurosurgical Section, Palo Alto Veterans Affairs Medical Center. Her research interests are in immunotherapy of brain tumors. She has been a strong advocate for changing the culture within schools of medicine to make them more hospitable institutions for the education and occupation of both women and minorities.

Jacalyn Duffin teaches history and philosophy of medicine at Queen's University in Kingston, Canada. Her research is nineteenth-century medicine and medical epistemology, especially concepts of disease. She is the author of *Langstaff: A Nineteenth Century Medical Life* (University of Toronto Press, 1993) and is currently writing an intellectual biography of R. T. H. Laennec (1781–1826), inventor of the stethoscope.

Janet Bickel enjoys the national networking opportunities possible as Assistant Vice President for Institutional Planning and Development and Director of Women's Programs at the Association of American Medical Colleges (AAMC). She has spoken on faculty professional development issues at more than thirty-five medical schools and published articles on a broad spectrum of areas in academic medicine, including student ethical development, tenure policies, part-time faculty appointments, parental leave, and leadership skill development She began her involvement with medical education at Brown University, where from 1972 to 1976 she served as admissions, financial aid and student affairs officer for the new medical school. She earned a M.A. in sociology while at Brown after graduating Phil Beta Kappa from the University of Missouri-Columbia with an A.B. in English. For the last eight years, she has also served as faculty for George Washington University School of Medicine and Health Sciences' Issues in Health Care course.

Kate Brown is an Associate Professor in the Center for Health Policy and Ethics at Creighton University, Omaha, Nebraska. A medical anthropologist, her research examines the relationship of sociocultural factors and human responses to illness and disease. Specifically, she is interested in the influence of gender, social class, ethnicity, and professional training on ethical decision-making and health care policy. For the School of Medicine she designed and taught a required ethics and policy course titled "An Ethic of Service: Contemporary Challenges and Opportunities in Medical Practice."

Leah J. Dickstein began her career teaching, first as an elementary school teacher in inner city Brooklyn, then as a Berlitz English language teacher in Ghent, Belgium, for three years. She received her medical degree from he University of Louisville in 1970, and is currently a professor in the Department of

Psychiatry and Behavioral Sciences, and the Associate Dean for Faculty and Student Advocacy at the University of Louisville School of Medicine. She has been vice-president of the American Psychiatric Association, and has been president of the American Medical Women's Association, the largest organization of women healthcare providers in the United States.

Marian Gray Secundy is Professor and Director of the Program in Medical Ethics at Howard University College of Medicine. She has been a Visiting Scholar at the University of San Francisco Health Policy Institute, the University of Chicago's Pritzker School of Medicine, the National Leadership Training Program in Clinical Medical Ethics, Michigan State University, and Hiram College. A practicing psychotherapist, Dr. Secundy is also editor of *Trials, Tribulations, and Celebrations: African-American Perspectives on Health, Illness, Aging, and Loss*. She served in 1993 as co-chair of the Ethics Working Group of Hillary Rodham Clinton's Health Care Task Force.

Marjorie Sirridge is Professor of Medicine and Director of the Office of Medical Humanities at the University of Missouri-Kansas City School of Medicine. She has enjoyed the practice and teaching of clinical medicine for forty years and was one of the founding faculty members of the UMKC School of Medicine in 1971. In the last four years she has taught courses in Literature and Medicine to medical students. Her current interest is in autobiographies of women physicians, including those of many of the courageous pioneers of the nineteenth century.

Mary Biody Mahowald is a Professor in the Department of Obstetrics and Gynecology at the University of Chicago and in its Center for Clinical Medical Ethics. Her books include *An Idealistic Pragmatism* (Nijhoff), *Philosophy of Woman* (Hackett), and *Women and Children in Health Care: An Unequal Majority* (Oxford). Currently she is concluding a three-year grant to study the impact of the human genome project on women, and commencing a two-year project to prepare primary caregivers to deal with the ethical and social implications of the new genetics.

Pamela Charney is an Associate Professor of Internal Medicine and an Assistant Professor of Obstetrics and Gynecology at the Albert Einstein College of Medicine in New York City. She is a general internist whose clinical activities are based at Jacobi Medical Center, a public hospital in the Bronx. Her teaching activities have included developing interactive educational programs for residents, medical students and faculty

Perri Klass is a pediatrician in Boston. She is the author of novels, short stories, and essays, including *A Not Entirely Benign Procedure, Other Women's Chil-*

dren, Baby Doctor, and *Taking Care of Your Own.* She was graduated from Harvard Medical School in 1986 and lives with her family in Cambridge, Massachusetts.

Rebekah Wang-Cheng teaches and practices general internal medicine at the Medical College of Wisconsin in Milwaukee where she is an Associate Professor of Medicine. She lectures and publishes on topics related to women's health, biopsychosocial medicine, and medical education, particularly the role of gender in performance evaluation of medical learners. She writes a biweekly question/answer column in the *Milwaukee Journal-Sentinel* newspaper.

Index